In Case You Teach English

An Interactive Casebook for Prospective and Practicing Teachers

Larry R. Johannessen
Northern Illinois University
DeKalb, Illinois

Thomas M. McCann
Community High School
West Chicago, Illinois

Merrill
Prentice Hall

Upper Saddle River, New Jersey
Columbus, Ohio

Library of Congress Cataloging-in-Publication Data

Johannessen, Larry R.

    In case you teach English : an interactive casebook for prospective and practicing teachers/Larry R. Johannessen, Thomas M. McCann.

       p. cm.

    Includes bibliographical references.

    ISBN 0-13-062310-5

    1. Case method. 2. English teachers—Training of. 3. English language—study and teaching. I. McCann, Thomas M. II. Title.

LB1029.C37 J64 2002

428′.0071—dc21

                                    2001034306

Vice President and Publisher: Jeffrey W. Johnston
Editor: Linda Montgomery
Managing Editor: Allyson P. Sharp
Production Editor: Mary M. Irvin
Design Coordinator: Diane C. Lorenzo
Text Design: Carlisle Publishers Services
Cover Design: Ali Mohrman
Cover Art: Ali Mohrman
Production Manager: Pamela D. Bennett
Director of Marketing: Kevin Flanagan
Marketing Manager: Krista Groshong
Marketing Coordinator: Barbara Koontz

This book was set in Berkeley by Carlisle Communications, Ltd., and was printed and bound by R. R. Donnelly & Sons Company. The cover was printed by Phoenix Color Corp.

Pearson Education Ltd., *London*
Pearson Education Australia Pty. Limited, *Sydney*
Pearson Education Singapore Pte. Ltd.
Pearson Education North Asia Ltd., *Hong Kong*
Pearson Education Canada, Ltd., *Toronto*
Pearson Educación de Mexico, S.A. de C.V.
Pearson Education—Japan, *Tokyo*
Pearson Education Malaysia Pte. Ltd.
Pearson Education, *Upper Saddle River, New Jersey*

10 9 8 7 6 5 4 3 2 1
ISBN 0-13-062310-5

We dedicate this book to
George Hillocks, Jr.—English teacher,
teacher educator, scholar, mentor, and friend.

Preface

As we were writing this book over the last two years, we interviewed several beginning teachers, held formal conferences with dozens of new and experienced teachers, and engaged in innumerable casual conversations with a variety of teachers. In addition, we surveyed preservice teachers about their expectations for their impending careers. Two themes emerged from our research: Preservice teachers are anxious about what is about to happen to them as they enter the profession; and many new teachers suffer a great deal as they try to navigate the tricky waters of becoming a professional educator. We know many teachers. We believe that teaching is a significant undertaking, with long-lasting effects on individuals and communities. We cannot afford to lose talented teachers because they were ill-equipped to contend with the challenges, annoyances, and frustrations that can grow into career-ending episodes. We hope that this modest effort in some way equips teachers with the strategic stepping-stones to help them to avoid disaster. In short, we hope to reduce the suffering and keep talented teachers in the profession.

FOCUS OF THE TEXT

A characteristic feature of the casebook is that it requires the user to interact with others. The strength of the casebook lies in using the text with other critical thinkers. Unlike a self-help book that prescribes practices, the casebook invites the user to engage with others in exploring possible responses to troubling situations. Our own experience as teachers tells us that learners develop some valuable habits of mind when they immerse themselves in significant conversations about issues that have relevance to their lives. The discussion reveals that reasonable people can see the same issue in astoundingly different ways. The variety of opinions exposes the possibilities. Challenges and questions prompt the thinker to use logic. Thinkers who develop a model for reasoning learn to support claims by providing grounds, to consider exceptions to generalizations, to represent fairly the opposing views, and to assess the alternative opinions. A series of conversations about some compelling cases highlights the image that teachers do not have to labor in isolation; in fact, we hope that readers will realize that the most satisfying and productive way to function as a teacher is to proceed in concert with others.

Each case in this book portrays as realistically as possible the tangled network of possibilities and considerations that necessarily infuse any thorny teaching experience. We hope to make the situations tough, and we want to pressure the readers of the book to make the hard choices. Experience tells us that difficult teaching situations are tough because there are factors that constrain us, and alternative perspectives that challenge us.

We contend that the use of this casebook will promote critical thinking. Our understanding of critical thinking involves the recognition of multiple points of view or the identification of several courses of action. Critical thinking necessarily involves the assessment of the relative merits of the points of view or the courses of action. In many instances, the assessment involves the weighing of advantages and disadvantages associated with each choice. With practice, the reader of the casebook will develop the habits of the critical and strategic thinker who can reasonably project the likely consequences for choices and embrace the choices that will promote the greatest benefit and cause the least damage.

ORGANIZATION OF THE TEXT

We understand that instructors may not want to assign their students to study all of the twenty cases included in the book. We have included a Grade and Issues Matrix inside the front cover to support the selection of the cases that might be the focus of a group's discussion. In this sense, the book is nonlinear. There is no need to progress from Case 1 to Case 20. The readers will pick and choose cases, guided by their particular goals, philosophical perspectives, and particular teaching contexts. We hope that we have included a sufficient variety of teaching environments as well as critical issues.

We have tried to support the efforts of the students who have been asked to study the text. As we would with our own students when we assign reading, we provide a preview and suggest some focus questions to guide study. The cases themselves tell a story, placing the reader in the position of the troubled character, prompting the participant to take some action. We offer a set of questions to guide discussion, but we recognize that after one initiates discussion of the cases, the discussion has its own momentum and does not require a prescribed set of prompts. We have suggested a few related research and writing projects as an extension of the thinking about each case. Instructors will likely suggest their own topics and modes of research as well.

On many occasions when we field-tested the cases, discussion participants shared related stories. Reviewers of early versions of the text observed that the twenty cases reminded them of at least fifty others from their own experiences. We guess that the reader has some compelling teaching stories to tell, or soon will have some. The twenty cases included in this book obviously do not exhaust the challenges that might beset an English teacher. For those who have a story to tell, we recommend a framework for composing the story in a way that will make it a powerful instructional tool. We hope that the book encourages readers to tell their own stories and suggests the importance of listening sympathetically to the stories of others.

ACKNOWLEDGMENTS

First, we would like to thank Dan C. Lortie, who taught us using the case study method developed at Harvard and showed us the value of case studies in teacher education. We would also like to thank George Hillocks, Jr., who taught us how to teach and what reflection-in-action really means. It is important that we thank Robert Small and Joseph Strzepek, whose groundbreaking casebook for preservice English teachers opened the door for our work. We would also like to thank our students and colleagues who have contributed in numerous ways, especially for the real-life teaching problems that were the inspiration for some of these cases. For their support, encouragement, critical comments, and wise counsel, our thanks go to Peter Smagorinsky, Elizabeth Kahn, Joe Flanagan, Pamela Gentile McCann, Jody O'Connell, John VonKerens, and Dianne Chambers. We also recognize the significant technical contributions Barney Ricca provided in the preparation of the manuscript. We would also like to thank the many pre-service and practicing teachers who allowed us to field-test our cases with them.

We would also like to thank the reviewers of this book for their helpful comments and suggestions: Peggy Albers, Georgia State University; Anna Bolling, California State University—Stanislaus; John Bushman, University of Kansas; Todd Goodson, Kansas State University; Patricia Kelly, Virginia Tech; and Wayne Slater, University of Maryland. We also very much appreciate our editors, especially Allyson Sharp and Lea Baranowski, for their support and encouragement throughout the development, writing, and production of the book and for their insights into both English education as a discipline and current needs in the market.

Foreword

Peter Smagorinsky
University of Georgia

University teacher education programs are often criticized for being "too theoretical" or "out of touch." Teachers "in the trenches" have often complained that university education professors are overly concerned with the latest theories and oblivious to how those theories work when the maintenance crew is repairing a radiator in the middle of class. What university teacher educators need to do, say the teachers, is concentrate less on the ideal classroom and help prepare prospective teachers for real ones.

These criticisms are not without grounds. A few years ago I studied the ways in which English education teaching methods are taught (Smagorinsky & Whiting, 1995), which required a reading of the many books that prospective teachers are assigned to read during their university coursework. One thing that stood out was the way in which so many of these books described teaching as relatively unproblematic. Kids can't write? Just have them keep journals and watch their writing blossom. Problems with discipline? Here are five rules for maintaining an orderly classroom. Students' writing is careless and ungrammatical? The problem is with your assignments; just let them pick their own topics and they'll care enough to make their writing presentable. All too often, these books suggest that teaching isn't so difficult if only you know the proper techniques.

I don't wish to diminish the importance of theory or technique; heaven help you if haven't got any. But teaching is also a matter of judgment. Judgment includes the knowledge of when and where to use particular techniques. It also involves the wisdom of how to conduct oneself in the myriad of complex situations, both educational and social, in which teachers are engaged every day. How can prospective teachers be prepared for these infinitely perplexing and challenging occasions that share only their inevitability? And, in particular, how can this happen in the relatively pristine environment of the university, where classes don't include members of rival street gangs who don't want to work in cooperative groups together?

Often such realities are viewed as the province of the practicum or student teaching; here, prospective teachers enter the school itself and have the opportunity to work with students in their native habitat. At times this foray into the classroom can be a shock: Students are distracted by the fthwat! fthwat! of water from the sprinkler slapping against the windows, a parent is outside the classroom door angry over a bad grade issued to her son, colleagues are engaged in territorial disputes about who teaches what at which grade level, the principal is building credentials to move up the career ladder and insisting on higher test scores at any cost, a student is suspended according to the school's zero-tolerance weapons policy for having a can opener in her purse, the school band is practicing off-tune in the room next door, students are answering cell phone calls in class, pranksters have pulled the fire alarms three times by the first lunch shift, . . . and it's only Monday. How on earth can someone be prepared to think about being an effective teacher, in all capacities and under all circumstances, through coursework in the relatively serene environment of the college classroom?

One way to help prepare prospective teachers for the realities of school is to keep reading when you're done with this Foreword and not stop until you reach the end of this book. Larry Johannessen and Tom McCann have provided a well-conceived set of cases to consider that will help teachers anticipate the kinds of problems that make life in school endlessly challenging. As a former teacher of 14 years, I can easily resonate with the dilemmas they raise for consideration in this book. In these pages, issues of curriculum and instruction, office politics, school climate, school and community citizenship, and much more are covered across the span of middle and secondary school English instruction.

This book is bound to be useful in a number of ways. First of all, it provides a simulated context for applying the theories and practices that are typically presented unproblematically in books about teaching English. As the authors note, the cases serve the same purpose as other simulations experienced by people learning to fly and drive, other occupations with serious consequences for on-the-job mistakes. And because these cases are grounded in the authors' ample experiences as public school teachers, they have the ring of truth for those who understand the profession. Indeed, I think this book should be required reading for anyone in the public dialogue who believes that solutions to educational problems are simple and easily implemented.

Another attribute is the open-ended nature of the cases. Teachers do not face problems with true/false or multiple choice answers. When a parent shows up, unannounced, to complain about vulgar language in an assigned novel, and the clock is ticking toward the beginning of class while the teacher desperately needs a trip to the washroom, any number of actions are possible. And many of these possibilities will create new problems that dwarf the original one in magnitude, yet a solution, or at least an action, is necessary right now. What to do? The solutions offered in a university classroom allow for greater deliberation and more input than is possible under the glare of an angry parent and the weight of a bulging bladder. However, that opportunity for extended consideration is also among the strengths offered by discussion of these cases. What to do, what to do? Students have the chance to contextualize the case in terms of their prior knowledge of schools and social interaction, to generate possible actions, to consider their consequences, to listen to opposing viewpoints, to reconsider their options, to consider the range of reverberations for various choices, and otherwise to think through how to act in a vexing, conflict-ridden, open-ended situation. Then, in the inevitable likelihood that they find themselves in similar circumstances, they will have rehearsed the possible outcomes of various courses of action and anticipate, to the greatest degree possible, what will follow from their choices.

Johannessen and McCann do an excellent job of framing the cases and providing ways in which to think about them. Each case is preceded by a preview of the problem type and a more specific focus for the particular problem occurring in the case. The cases themselves, while seemingly brief, include the necessary detail to make them difficult to resolve. Following each case is a request for a solution, a set of ancillary questions for discussion, and suggested further reading and writing relative to the case. While discussion facilitators are welcome to take different approaches to considering the cases than that recommended by the authors, it's useful to provide this support for independent readers of the book and instructors who prefer a structured approach to analyzing the problems.

This is the first casebook for English teachers since Small and Strzepek's (1988) collection. It is a most welcome addition to the field of the scholarship of teaching, one that I look forward to using with my own students.

REFERENCES

Smagorinsky, P., & Whiting, M. E. (1995). *How English teachers get taught: Methods of teaching the methods class.* Urbana, IL: Conference on English Education and National Council of Teachers of English.

Small, R. C., & Strzepek, J. E. (1988). *A casebook for English teachers: Dilemmas and decisions.* Belmont, CA: Wadsworth.

Contents

The Case for the Use of Case Studies

We had no idea what to expect at the annual fall conference of the Illinois Association of Teachers of English when we agreed to co-chair a session for new teachers to talk about their struggles and successes. However, as we started the session, we were pleased that there were more than 20 people from around the state sitting in a semicircle around the room. We asked the participants to introduce themselves and describe where they taught. There were a number of first- and second-year teachers, two or three teachers in the midst of student teaching, a few preservice teachers, and even a few experienced teachers who had come to offer guidance for the new initiates into the profession and discuss some of their own concerns. When we asked the teachers to discuss their problems and struggles, it was as if we had opened up a floodgate.

One first-year teacher talked about how overwhelmed she felt with her teaching and coaching responsibilities. As she put it, "I knew it was going to be hard the first year, but I didn't realize that I wasn't going to have time for anything else. I mean," she said in exasperation, "I don't have any kind of personal life at all."

Another new teacher talked about the problems she was having with the girls on her cheerleading squad: "I guess I didn't know that many of these kids don't have adults around that they can talk to about their problems. They bring all of their personal problems to me, and I really don't feel prepared for dealing with them."

Another first-year teacher talked about how difficult it was for him with four different course preparations and all the planning involved and trying to get all of his papers graded and back to his students in a reasonable amount of time. "I feel very guilty," he said. "I go home, eat dinner, plan my courses for the next day, and then grade papers. Sometimes I fall asleep at my desk at home grading papers. I know I should be getting their papers back to them in a week, but I just can't do it. I feel guilty all the time. I've had some of their papers for almost a month."

Another teacher talked about how difficult it was for her to put into practice the ideas and methods that she had learned in her teacher education program: "They handed me a set of books and a curriculum guide at my school and said, 'Teach it.' I know that some of what I have been doing isn't very good, but I don't even know who to talk to about trying something different."

One of the more experienced teachers in the group noted that he had a similar problem at his school. "No one seems to want to try anything new or different. It seems like I've been talking with my colleagues for years just to get them to add one or two young adult novels to the literature curriculum."

A new teacher who seemed particularly distraught talked about how upset she was because one of her students had called her a "bitch." "I grew up and attended this high school in this small town," she said. "I can't believe that she would say that to me."

Finally, a student teacher expressed concern about the lack of respect she experienced from her students and even some of her colleagues. "I know I look and dress young," she said, "but every time I walk down the hall, someone asks me for my hall pass. What can I do to get my students and colleagues to respect me?"

As the session progressed, and we discussed the problems and issues raised by the group and explored possible solutions that these teachers might try in their situations, it became very clear to the two of us that all of the new teachers really appreciated the opportunity to discuss these issues. At one point, one new teacher commented that it was gratifying for her to hear a veteran teacher say that he had difficulties making judgments about grades for student work. She had assumed that experienced teachers didn't wrestle with these issues.

The session revealed to us that every English teacher, whether new or experienced, must confront a variety of issues and problems in his or her teaching career, and, while we all benefited from the give-and-take discussion that took place at this session of this conference, teachers could benefit even more if they were to receive some formal training in solving the kinds of problems they are likely to encounter in their teaching careers. This conference session, then, highlighted the need for, and suggested the possible value of, case study analysis in teacher education.

Any reflective person will gain some knowledge and understanding from experience. Anyone who has experienced a troublesome situation might be able, in retrospect, to identify alternative courses of action or to weigh the true gravity of a problem. There is obviously no substitute for experience; however, when one is able to simulate an experience realistically, then the actual experience itself seems less threatening and the practitioner learns some problem-solving strategies, which he or she can apply to new challenges. This is the expectation that guides the use of flight simulators for pilots in training and the use of automobile simulators for novice drivers. The same sort of thinking invites active learners to engage with others in analyzing problems and discussing the possibilities for action. Case study analysis is a common practice in graduate business schools, in law schools, and in leadership training. Both novice and veteran teachers can gain much through the process of deliberating about how to work through difficult situations. Every tough situation that the teacher endures prepares one to deal constructively with similar encounters.

This text offers 20 cases for study and discussion. The cases introduce a variety of problem-based situations that could very easily confront an English teacher during the course of a career. Each case has the following characteristics:

- *Immediacy:* The case suggests some urgency to decide and act, so there is limited time to ponder, research, discuss, and select a course of action.

- *Action:* The case prompts discussants to deliberate and take specific action.
- *Detail:* The case provides sufficient description of the complicating factors and competing perspectives.
- *Problem:* Each case poses such a challenge that it is not easy to find a simple solution and a completely satisfying response.

No Nightmares

The following collection of cases might give one the impression that the teaching of English is a prolonged nightmare, with each day presenting new and harrowing challenges. On the contrary, we expect that one's career in the teaching of English will be richly rewarding and that most days in the classroom will be pleasant. The cases presented here represent problem situations that we have experienced, or can imagine experiencing, over a 25-year career. We describe 20 cases. If one teaches for 25 years and experiences all of these problem situations, that is a rate of less than one problem per year. If one faced all of these challenges over the course of a career, that would mean fewer than one potential sleepless night each year. However, if one is not prepared for challenges and assumes that the world of teaching is a gentle place, with no controversy and little animosity, he or she may very well experience nightmares or "career-ending" decisions.

Becoming a Reflective Practitioner

Cooper and McNergney (1995) argue that case studies help students of teaching to think like teachers because work with the cases provides preservice teachers with practice; they are "opportunities to encounter real teaching problems in the safety and security of simulated situations" where teachers can try out principles of teaching and learning without causing any harm to themselves or others in the process. Drawing on experiences in other fields and some work in education, Merseth (1991) maintains that there are several benefits to be derived from applying case methods to teacher education programs:

1. Case-based instruction helps students develop skills of critical analysis and problem solving. The use of cases of teaching experiences can help students observe closely, make inferences, identify relationships, and articulate organizing principles. As Merseth observes, "Cases send a powerful message that teaching is complex, contextual, and reflexive" (p. 16).
2. The case method of instruction encourages reflective practice and deliberate action by encouraging students to discuss and choose from among competing interpretations and solutions advanced by one another. This process is in line with Donald Schon's and John Dewey's vision of "reflection-in-action."
3. Cases help students analyze and make decisions in complex situations that may not be a perfect match between theory and practice. As Merseth indicates, working with cases brings "chunks of reality" into the classroom, and they expose students to settings and contexts that would normally not be available.

4. The case method creates an environment for active learning. It involves students in their own learning. Students cannot sit back passively, as they might in a lecture situation; they must actively participate in the learning that takes place.
5. Cases tend to generate lively and engaging discussions. Students have the opportunity to begin assuming the role of teacher as they share their own knowledge and begin taking responsibility for their own learning as they express their own understanding, values, opinions, and interpretations about teaching.
6. The case approach encourages the formation of a community of learners. By taking responsibility for their own learning as well as contributing to the learning of others, students learn to work together in teams.

There is precious little research on the use of case-method teaching in teacher education. However, Sykes and Bird (1992) and Grossman (1992), drawing on research by Spiro et al. (1987), conclude that case methods may be best suited for learning in areas that could be described as "ill-structured domains." A key feature of such domains is ambiguity; they are domains in which relevent knowledge is not organized to fit a specific situation. As Grossman argues, "The value of cases for teacher education lies in their potential to represent the messy world of practice, to stimulate problem solving in a realm in which neither the problem nor the solution is clear" (p. 237). Teaching is an ill-structured domain, and English teaching might be the most ill-structured, or messiest, of them all. Each day of English teaching, events unfold differently, and teachers must orchestrate a dizzying array of factors to encourage learning. Spiro and his colleagues (1988) argue that just learning general principles is not enough to help students learn how to operate effectively in ill-structured domains, but the "structured dynamics of cases" are key to helping students learn how to apply the principles or how to "reason from precedent cases" in such domains; the cases are absolutely necessary because they are the examples of the "abstract principles" (p. 379).

Finally, one of the most compelling arguments for using cases to prepare teachers, especially English teachers, is that they relate good stories. Cooper and McNergney (1995) state, "Stories are powerful and easier to remember than decontextualized information, and they seem to 'fit' with teachers' ways of organizing their knowledge of teaching" (p. 5). If this is true for teachers in general, then it is particularly true for English teachers. Stories are our stock-in-trade. We hope that these cases or stories help the developing teachers to learn how to use important principles in their teaching and to become more reflective practitioners.

SELECTION OF CASES

We have relied on memories of our own experiences and the witnessing of daily crises to generate a list of case topics. To narrow our choices, we have relied on research about *teacher concerns.* The influential work of Fuller (1969), and later of Rutherford and Hall (1990), reveals that beginning teachers have serious concerns about managing classrooms, about being viewed as a credible professional by their colleagues and by parents, about being liked and accepted by students, and about being evaluated by supervisors.

We also know from our own experience with general methods classes and English methods classes that preservice teachers also worry about how they will grade students, how they will respond to challenges about grades, and how they will handle a monumental workload. Pre-service teachers also commonly express concerns about having the freedom to put into practice the concepts and beliefs about teaching that they have embraced during their college or university training. We expect that the case studies will allow beginning teachers to face their apprehension and work with others to arrive at some strategies to make the prospect of problems less intimidating.

We have provided a variety of cases: from logistical difficulties to moral dilemmas. We have tried to avoid the mundane and the sensational. Every teacher will encounter some disagreeable students and face some classroom management obstacles. Mentors, supervisors, and administrators should be able to advise and support a teacher about these problems. Schools could face more serious problems, such as earthquakes, fire, asteroid collision, or terrorist attack, but the chances of a teacher's experiencing one of these disasters are slim, and our deliberations would be futile in the face of such catastrophes. We are left with the fairly complicated cases that one could face every year. We invite the reader to examine and discuss cases that present problems worth discussing. They are worth discussing in the sense that a teacher could benefit from thinking through the conditions and ramifications with other reasonable persons. We hope that practice with some of the cases helps one develop strategies and habits of thinking that will serve the teacher in times of crisis, so that challenges remain challenges and don't become nightmares.

AUDIENCE FOR THIS TEXT

We hope that the discussion and reflection about the cases in this text support all English teachers, whether they have 20 years of experience or 6 months. These cases fit naturally into the undergraduate and graduate preservice and inservice English education curriculum. In the real world of English teaching, teachers must be prepared to handle unanticipated situations, to adapt current knowledge to deal with new problems, and to learn radically new things. In other words, English teachers must be able to deal constructively with change. In order to prepare English teachers to act creatively and intelligently in the classroom, preservice and inservice courses, workshops, and programs must become training laboratories where real teaching situations are confronted, pondered, and acted upon. Participants must have the opportunity to bridge the gap between theory and practice. In order to become thoughtful and creative problem solvers, participants need practice in analyzing problems, in asking important questions, in considering a variety of responses, in arguing for or against different solutions or possible courses of action, and in seeking more than one answer to a problem. To be successful, English teachers must constantly think through problems and arrive at appropriate solutions. As Donald Schon (1983) insists, "Teaching is a profession that demands reflection in action." Cases help learners understand concepts by actually experiencing them, by figuring them out for themselves, by holding them in their hands, by grappling with their nuances and subtleties, and by testing solutions in an environment that encourages diverse perspectives.

Our teaching experience and primary interests lie in the teaching of English; consequently, we have developed cases that feature situations that are common to the English teacher. Some cases raise issues that hold special interest for English teachers. Other cases represent experiences that could confront any teacher, no matter what grade or subject. We include a case and issues matrix so that the users of the text can select those cases that have relevance and currency for the particular course of study or professional development goals. Any teacher might benefit from studying the cases. Problems arise in schools all the time; the problems become crises when they take the teacher by surprise and he or she is ill equipped to think strategically about the problems. Problems that grow unchecked have the dangerous potential to absorb one's time and attention, distracting the teacher from the instructional program that brings the joys and energy to our profession.

TOPICS AND FORMAT FOR THE CASES

The text provides narratives and an analytical framework for 20 cases. Many of the cases raise policy issues; some of the cases offer procedural challenges. With the use of all the cases, conversation is an essential part of the process of working toward a resolution. It is worthwhile for any teacher to recognize that in education one functions as part of a community, and constructive solutions and policies derive from collaborative discourse.

Each case begins with a preview, which includes a summary and a series of focus questions. The case narrative and related artifacts follow. A format for discussion guides deliberation. The discussion questions vary with the specific needs and details of the particular case. The following examples represent the kind of considerations that will guide reflection and discussion:

- What are the central issues in the case? If there is a controversy, what are the competing sides in the case?
- If the case poses a management problem, what are the particular constraints or specifications that you must meet?
- If the case raises a policy question, identify the needs that must be met, or the harms that should be reduced or eliminated.
- For each possible course of action, identify the likely benefits and potential disadvantages.
- If applicable, identify short-term and long-term solutions to the problem. Be prepared to explain your plan in detail.
- What are the merits of the views of each side in the controversy?
- To what extent does the case represent a political problem? In what sense are various parties competing for limited resources?
- Can you characterize the case as a structural problem that demands the careful design of organizational structures or mechanisms?
- To what extent does the case require the management of symbols that can spark emotional responses?

FIELD-TESTING THE CASES

The cases have been field-tested with preservice and practicing teachers. After using each case, we asked the discussion participants to complete an evaluation of the case as an instructional activity. The evaluation instrument appears as an appendix to this text and might be useful to an instructor in judging the effectiveness of selected cases as a means for exploring key educational issues.

When we introduced the cases to students in undergraduate English methods and curriculum classes and in graduate education classes, the cases prompted animated discussion, with wide participation. The reaction to the use of the cases was consistently positive. First of all, the cases always produced discussion. One preservice teacher noted, "I felt there was a great deal of meaningful discussion raised among the class." Another person in the class stated, "It made us discuss a lot. There was a lot of controversy about what should happen to the teacher." Discussion participants noted that the deliberation about the case revealed a variety of perspectives about the critical issues. One student observed the following about a case dealing with grading: "Class not only debated on whether these students should pass or not, but also on what the teacher should do in the future and what his mistakes were." The problematic or controversial nature of each case created a class dynamic that invited the investment of each participant and revealed several opposing views. One student observed, "The class ended up having a heated debate about what the teacher should do."

We know that the cases will generate lively discussions, but what is the value of such discussion? In response to one case, a student observed, "It opened my eyes to things that teachers really have to deal with." The users of the cases testify that the details of the cases and the discussions about them expose novices to many unanticipated but crucial issues—some that are seemingly mundane and pragmatic challenges, others that are moral and ethical dilemmas. Discussion participants have commonly pointed out that the deliberation about each case exposed them to some issues and potential problems that they had previously been unaware of. One person reported, "I believe the thought that goes into the factors of the case study and the discussion among students afterward are both valuable to future teachers in helping them decide how they might handle similar situations." The participants expressed a belief that the thinking that they applied to the current case could transfer to new situations: "It helps you to think about the type of problem solving you will constantly be doing as a teacher and plan for some of those issues."

Consistently, the novice teachers testify to the value of discussing the cases: "I think that this really would help prospective teachers because this shows them what other teachers go through and what they may go through." In response to a case about grading, one discussion participant noted, "This is a great case study for practicing teachers in showing them how communication between students, parents, and teachers should be done." Another participant reported a typical response: "The value of this case is immense. We as pre-service teachers should be asked to reflect on meaningful material."

Our experience in using the cases with prospective and practicing teachers suggests that the cases are powerful instruments for preparing teachers for future challenges and for encouraging them to reflect on current practices.

NOTE TO THE PROFESSOR OR FACILITATOR

Deliberation about each case will be most productive if each participant initially studies the case independently. Introductory questions can guide the reading. The facilitator might find it useful to have participants discuss the case in pairs or in small groups. In this way, everyone contributes insights and suggestions. Another phase of the process would involve a larger group of participants in discussion. The large-group discussion exposes multiple perspectives and a variety of possible actions.

In no instance do we offer the "correct" answer for the problems posed by the case. Involvement in the case trains teachers in reflecting about difficult issues. Instead of progressing toward a correct answer, the facilitator guides the participants in refining analytical procedures. This means that the facilitator will ask discussants to explain, support, and project: Why does someone make a particular claim? What are the logical consequences connected to taking certain actions? Are there any exceptions to one's generalizations? Does a proposal stand up to tests under particular circumstances? Who would disagree? What are the merits and shortcomings of the opposing views?

Sometimes discussion will be frustrating because some issues are so elusive and contentious that they do not permit satisfying solutions. As sometimes occurs on the job, deliberation can end abruptly when a situation requires immediate action. In the end, the users of the cases should recognize that the text provides no answer key. Some discussants will find it frustrating that a tangible correct answer eludes them, and it will be difficult for a facilitator to bring a discussion to closure. Instead of pursuing the correct answer, a discussion leader should look for reasonable analyses and the expression of strategic plans for confronting similar situations in the future.

Typically a person who facilitates discussion about a case study follows these practices:

1. Allow the discussion participants time to prepare to discuss the case. In their preparation, the participants might find it productive to identify several possible courses of action, predict the likely result for each course of action, and weigh the benefits and disadvantages for each choice.
2. As the discussion begins and progresses, rely on frequent paraphrases of the participants' remarks, while avoiding evaluative comments. The other participants are likely to provide the challenges and evaluative comments to prompt a discussant to develop thought further.
3. Invite other participants to evaluate the analysis of previous speakers.
4. Press participants to be logical by posing appropriate follow-up questions: Why do you say that? What does that mean? How does that information support your claim?
5. Recognize that time constraints will dictate the need to bring a discussion to closure.

In the end, the facilitator would look for evidence that the participants have thought critically and strategically, in the sense that they have entertained multiple ways of looking at the problems and have made evaluation judgments about the most reasonable, ethical, and efficacious course of action. The facilitator can then summarize the essence of the discussion and perhaps prompt an informal written response or further research and writing.

POSTDISCUSSION PRODUCTS

There are two obvious possibilities for postdiscussion products. Some groups who work with a case might choose to play out the drama of the situation. In other words, after some preparation, the participants engage in role playing to see how the proposed solutions would work: for example, enact a meeting with a disgruntled parent or represent a debate with colleagues about a new approach to the teaching of reading. In some instances, the case will invite a written response. The specific case will suggest the form of, and audience for, the writing. In either case, taking some action after the discussion extends understanding of the controversy and allows the participant to project the likely consequences for one's decisions.

WRITING ONE'S OWN CASES

The 20 cases contained in this book cannot account for the dozens of difficult and frustrating situations that could emerge in a school every year. The instructor and other discussion participants who use this book might discover that they would like to write a case of their own and present it to colleagues for examination and analysis. Experience tells us that a case that stimulates meaningful discussion and promotes analytical thinking has some key features. This last section of the book (A Guide to Writing One's Own Cases) identifies these important features as a framework for producing new cases, which are not represented in the current text.

1 Surprise! We've Come to Complain

PREVIEW

How should teachers respond to parents' challenges about the literature that the teachers require the students to read? This case asks the reader to consider whether some challenges have any merit and legitimacy. Is it dangerous to allow any potential censor to have any influence? In the following case, a relatively inexperienced teacher faces parents' complaints about certain required reading. The teacher must prepare for a meeting with the parents and decide how to work with the student, who might feel uncomfortable with the current reading.

FOCUS QUESTIONS

As you read the following case, prepare to discuss these questions: (1) What planning should the teacher do for a meeting with parents who are voicing a complaint about the selection of literature? (2) How should the teacher treat the complaint and respond to the parents and to the student?

THE CASE

Surprise! We've Come to Complain

Lauren Saplin arrived at school early one Monday morning during her second year of teaching, so that she could finish some preparation before her first-period class. She had intended to put books on the desks and make a transparency with the directions for an activity her students would be doing during the first-period class. Lauren estimated that she would be able to complete her preparations and still have time to use the washroom before she had to teach two classes in a row. It was approximately 30 minutes before the first-period bell when Lauren approached her classroom and noticed two adults standing by the door. Lauren didn't recognize them as staff members. She thought, "Oh, no! I hope I didn't forget an appointment with someone's parents."

Lauren noticed that neither adult displayed the required visitor's pass, but she approached in her usual courteous manner: "Can I help you?"

"Are you Ms. Saplin?" the man asked. "I'm Oliver Carstead, and this is my wife, Amelia. Our daughter Louise is in your English class. If you have a couple of minutes, we'd like to talk to you about the reading you have assigned for your class."

"My first-period class meets soon," said Lauren, "but I can give you a few minutes now. Come on in."

Mr. and Mrs. Carstead sat down at desks in Lauren's room, and, before she could set her books down, they told her emphatically that they objected to her selection of Steinbeck's *Of Mice and Men* as assigned reading in a ninth-grade class. Mr. Carstead took the lead in describing his disgust at the appearance of profanities in the book. He opened the book and pointed to such words and phrases as *bastard, crap,* and *son of a bitch.* He also expressed concern that his daughter was exposed to the use of "the Lord's name in vain." Mr. Carstead showed Lauren instances in the text where characters uttered as expletives the words *Jesus* and *God damn.* The parents agreed that the most objectionable language of all was the repeated use of a racial slur and pointed to several appearances of the word *nigger* in the text. Mr. Carstead noted that his daughter Louise was the only African American student in the class, and he understood that it was Ms. Saplin's practice to read several passages from the novel aloud during her lessons. Mr. Carstead appeared to Lauren to be quite agitated when he described his concern that his daughter would be the object of curiosity, unwanted solicitude, or perhaps derision as the students read these offensive passages aloud in class. Mr. Carstead noted that he hadn't read the entire book but claimed that representative pages told him the nature and quality of the entire text.

Lauren explained that she had some flexibility in selecting material for her class and that she had selected *Of Mice and Men* because she believed that it taught students important lessons about friendship and alienation. She explained further that it was her hope that the reading and the discussing of the novel would serve as a tool to fight race prejudice and hatred.

The minutes ticked away until Lauren had to point out that her first-period class was about to begin. Mr. and Mrs. Carstead noted, "We are by no means done with this matter. We want to know what you are going to do about exposing children to this offensive book, and we want to know what you are going to do in regard to our daughter."

The first-period bell was about to ring when Lauren agreed to meet with the Carsteads after school the next day. Of course, it was a little difficult to concentrate on the lesson at hand after this encounter. A number of questions and considerations came to mind: How would she defend to the Carsteads her use of the novel in question and convince them that it has some merit as a literary work? Should she bring other people to the meeting or meet with the Carsteads alone? How should she treat Louise Carstead? Lauren recalled that Louise commented in class that she had already completed reading the novel. In some sense, then, the Carsteads' challenge seemed too late, and there seemed to be nothing that Lauren could do now. If Lauren were to excuse Louise from any lessons related to the novel, the separation would surely call attention to the girl and make her feel more uncomfortable. If Louise were excused from the current lessons, what would she do while the other students worked with the novel? Lauren tried to remember how she had introduced the novel. She couldn't recall if she had warned the students about the language. How could she explain the fact that she had exposed students to profanities without warning them?

If you were in Lauren Saplin's position, what would you do? What would you do when you saw Louise Carstead in your afternoon class? What would you do in preparation for tomorrow's meeting? What provisions or policy changes, if any, would you make in the future?

QUESTIONS FOR DISCUSSION

1. Has Lauren made any errors in selecting the text, in reading parts out loud in class, or in requiring that everyone read it? Explain.
2. Is there anything that Lauren can do to ease Louise's discomfort in the class? Should Lauren make any exceptions for Louise? Why?
3. How can Lauren justify requiring her students to read a book which contains profanities and ethnic slurs?
4. To what extent would it benefit Lauren to include other persons besides the Carsteads at their meeting? Should she involve other persons, whether or not they actually attend the meeting?
5. What do you expect will occur at the meeting? What do you think the parents want? What concessions, if any, do you think Lauren should be willing to make?
6. What would you recommend as Lauren's plan for the next 36 hours? What are the benefits and possible disadvantages to your plan?
7. In the long term, what would you recommend that Lauren do? What would be the benefits to this long-term plan? In the end, what disadvantages can you predict will result from your plan? Can you show that, on balance, your recommended course of action will probably result in more benefits than problems?

RELATED RESEARCH AND WRITING

Research *one* of the following topics, prepare a written report, and share your findings with your colleagues.

1. Consult publications from the National Council of Teachers of English (NCTE) or the American Library Association (ALA) to learn which books are most often challenged. What are the most common bases for the challenges? What help can NCTE and ALA provide for teachers and librarians who wish to include some of the challenged titles as part of the literature curriculum or the school collection? Useful resources will be NCTE's website at http://www.ncte.org/censorship, and the ALA's website at http://www.ala.org/alaorg/oif/.
2. Read about one case of a censorship challenge in a school in your area or in the area where you hope to work in the future. What was the nature of the challenge? How did the teacher or the school respond to the challenge? What were some of the emotional aspects of the case? What was the final outcome?

3. From a list of commonly challenged books, identify one work that you could find yourself teaching in the future. Expect a challenge to your use of the book. What would be the likely arguments against your using the book? How would you respond to the challenges? What provisions could you make in your class and with the school administration, so that any censorship challenge does not escalate into a large-scale controversy?

2 *Pressure Cooker: Where Should We Devote Our Energies?*

PREVIEW

Casual observers of education mistakenly assume that teachers face a relatively easy task. Only the conscientious practitioners recognize how very exhausting teaching can be. In the following case, a young teacher can ease her burden by abdicating the coaching responsibilities that she finds the best part of her job. Many teachers, especially in the early years of their careers, face the challenge of balancing extracurricular activities with teaching duties. Any teaching position makes many demands on the teacher's resources and endurance. Each teacher must decide how to apportion his or her energies.

FOCUS QUESTIONS

As you read the following case, prepare to discuss these questions: (1) Should Sandi Demos continue with her coaching responsibilities? (2) How can Sandi balance her various responsibilities without damaging her health or compromising instructional integrity?

THE CASE

Pressure Cooker: Where Should We Devote Our Energies?

When Sandi Demos was hired at the same school where she had completed her student teaching, it was like a dream come true. During Sandi's student teaching at Claussen Community High School, South, her cooperating teacher was Dorothy Deiter. Mrs. Deiter had been at the school for 35 years and had served most of that time as the speech team coach. Dorothy Deiter—or Dottie, as she was affectionately known—was a legendary speech coach. Her teams filled a school trophy case with awards, including nine first-place performances at state competition and three first-place finishes at the national finals.

When Sandi was student teaching, she also assisted Mrs. Deiter with the speech team. Sandi chaperoned trips to tournaments, she judged selected speech events, and she actually did some coaching. The experience with the speech team was the highlight of Sandi's student teaching. She felt that she got to know the students personally and saw some talents that they seldom exhibited in the classroom. Sandi especially enjoyed her relationship with her mentor teacher. Dottie Deiter always managed to maintain a positive outlook, even under the most trying of circumstances. She appeared to have boundless energy and could always find time to talk to Sandi, whether it was about a lesson or a personal family matter. To Sandi, Dottie Deiter was more like a kindly aunt or a personal friend than a supervisor. Mrs. Deiter impressed Sandi as the ideal teacher. When Sandi was selected to replace Mrs. Deiter as both teacher and coach when Mrs. Deiter retired, it was a proud moment. It was apparent that Mrs. Deiter's recommendation carried significant influence in the choice of Sandi as a replacement. Sandi only hoped that she could in some small measure live up to the standard set by Dottie Deiter. To Sandi, her appointment as teacher and speech team coach seemed too good to be true.

By December, however, the euphoria of last spring seemed a shadowy and distant memory. Sandi was feeling overwhelmed. The combination of planning lessons, grading papers, attending to endless management duties, and coaching a speech team was incredibly taxing. Like everyone else at school, Sandi was hurried and fatigued. She no longer had time for regular exercise, she bolted her meals on the run, and she averaged about 4 hours of sleep per night.

On a typical day, Sandi arrived early at school to do some preparation, to expedite some paperwork, and to meet with individual students. She taught five classes, which required three different preparations. Like her colleagues, Sandi monitored the hallways during passing periods and for a portion of her preparation period. Sandi met her speech team members after school until about 6 o'clock. In the evening, Sandi spent 3 or 4 hours in preparation and in grading papers. Of course, most weekends in the fall were taken up with speech tournaments, which typically ran Friday evening and all day on Saturday.

The constant grind of teaching and coaching had a serious effect on Sandi's personal life. To her friends, she seemed sullen. When she excused herself from some social occasions with her friends, they thought that she was trying to avoid them. Her sister and parents found her uncharacteristically short-tempered and negative. Sandi's long-time boyfriend, Stuart, expressed concern that Sandi seemed to lose enthusiasm for going out and having fun. She even fell asleep twice on a date at the movie theater. The fatigue became especially alarming when Sandi dozed at the wheel and nearly ran the car off the road as she returned from school after a speech tournament.

By December, Sandi had serious doubts about herself. She wondered, "What is wrong with me that I can't keep up and manage things? Mrs. Deiter always seemed to take matters in stride and have abundant energy. Maybe I'm just not cut out to be a teacher."

When she shared her doubts with her parents, her father advised, "Why don't you just give up the coaching? You can't burn the candle at both ends. Your *teaching* is your job. The speech team is *extra*." Sandi couldn't bear the thought of giving up the speech team. With the strong speech tradition at Claussen, her selection as coach gave her immediate status and respect in the school and in the community. Her team this year had experienced considerable success, and she enjoyed being with the team. In fact, the only real joy she got out of her teaching position was her coaching experiences. Sandi told her parents, "If I give up coaching, I may as well give up teaching."

When Sandi confided her feelings to Stuart, this was his response: "Do you have to be Super Teacher of the Year? You take yourself too seriously. Don't assign so many papers. Give the kids a couple of days to just read in class, or have them do other stuff that you don't have to grade. Or just show some videos."

One of the veteran teachers at Claussen recognized Sandi's decline and suggested this: "Listen, kid. Whenever you're not feeling your best, take a 'mental health day.' You've got plenty of sick days. Just take a day off. The world will go on without you. Why make yourself sick by stretching yourself to the limit?"

To complicate matters for Sandi, she worried about the financial loss that she would suffer if she quit coaching. She was not getting rich as a speech coach, but every little bit helped. She knew she was attractive to the district because she could both coach and teach. She was nontenured, in a probationary period of her employment. The district could easily release her without cause if she stopped coaching. Sandi worried about the loss of a job. Claussen was one of the more affluent schools in the area, and it offered a very competitive salary schedule. She had recently bought her first new car, and she was eager to keep up the payments.

Sandi thought that she would take plenty of time during the school's winter break to get some rest and to reflect on her future. She had to decide first of all whether she was going to continue as speech team coach during the second semester, with a speech tournament season that ran until April. If she endured the current year, she had to decide if she would coach in the future. Sandi also had to decide if she was cut out to be a teacher. Could she go on teaching without the satisfaction she earned from coaching? **When Sandi returns to school after her winter break, what should she do?**

QUESTIONS FOR DISCUSSION

1. Is it reasonable to expect Sandi to give up her coaching responsibilities? If she gives up her coaching position, when should she resign? What are the positive and negative implications associated with the decision to resign?
2. Recall the advice that other persons offered Sandi. What did they advise? Assess the merits of each person's advice. Would you support any of these advisors?
3. Presumably, Sandi has entered into a contract with the school district to coach a team. Must she honor that contract, no matter what? Would a school district likely oppose her attempts to withdraw from her contractual responsibilities?
4. Does the coaching of a speech team carry as much weight as the coaching of a high-profile athletic team, such as varsity football or basketball? If there are any distinctions, how would they affect Sandi's decisions?
5. How vulnerable is Sandi in regard to losing her job? Realistically, would a school district release a teacher because she honestly felt that she could no longer coach? If this were the case, how could the teacher challenge the dismissal?
6. Devise a short-term and a long-term plan for Sandi. Through your analysis, show why your recommendations are the best plan for Sandi.

RELATED RESEARCH AND WRITING

Research *one* of the following topics, prepare a written report, and share your findings with your colleagues.

1. Talk to personnel directors, principals, or department chairs in several schools in your area or where you intend to work to determine if extracurricular responsibilities are a required part of a teacher's job. Are new teachers, especially, expected to take on a coaching or club supervision role? If extracurricular duties are part of the job description for a teacher, why does the school judge these duties to be an important part of the job?

2. Interview a teacher who is also a coach or club sponsor. How does the teacher handle the time-consuming extracurricular duties without allowing those responsibilities to interfere with the quality of his or her instruction?

3. Read some of the research about stress, school climate, and the effects these factors have on teacher morale. What are some of the dangers associated with the stresses teachers experience when their jobs demand long hours and confront them with various pressures? How do some veteran teachers manage the workload effectively? What strategies have teachers found to manage stress in a constructive and healthy way?

3

Killing the Boat People: Respect, Confidentiality, and Security

PREVIEW

In the following case, a situation challenges a teacher's pledge to respect confidentiality. The teacher must decide if something more is at stake than his promise to keep students' writing confidential. In the process, the teacher must decide if the ideas expressed in a student's writing constitute a genuine threat. At the same time, the teacher must determine if he has to respect the right of each student to harbor any thought he or she wishes, no matter how hateful or disturbing the teacher finds that thought.

FOCUS QUESTIONS

As you read the following case, prepare to discuss these questions: (1) Is there a real and immediate threat to anyone? (2) Must the teacher keep his pledge to maintain confidentiality? (3) In the end, what immediate and long-term actions should the teacher take?

THE CASE

Killing the Boat People: Respect, Confidentiality, and Security

On Sunday evening, Rodney Welkins immersed himself in his usual routine of reading students' "writer's logs" from the previous week. He wasn't exactly *grading papers* in the usual sense. Rodney had students keep a writer's log in his writer's workshop class as a means of collecting their thoughts and exploring ideas. Rodney gave students credit for this writing, but he felt that he couldn't grade the logs in the sense of *correcting* them or making evaluative judgments about their exploration of ideas. Instead, Rodney responded to the students and their writing in a personal way—by asking questions, by sharing similar thoughts, and by offering encouragement.

Rodney saw the students' use of the writer's logs and his responses to them as key elements in his approach to writing instruction. When Rodney introduced the writer's log concept to his students, he assured them that they could write anything they wanted, using whatever language and forms of written expression they desired. If the students' writing were to be genuine, honest, and fresh, insisted Rodney, the students must be free to choose topics and modes of writing that they valued and that represented who they were. Rodney earnestly hoped to avoid channeling students' efforts into producing the predictable party-line drivel that was intended only to satisfy the teacher. In the spirit of this approach, Rodney would have to honor a commitment to freedom and confidentiality: Students must have the freedom to say whatever they wanted in their logs, and Rodney must respect the privacy of their thoughts by not sharing the students' writing with parents, colleagues, and school administrators without the writer's permission. In the past, some students had tested Rodney's resolve to allow freedom of expression and to keep their work confidential. Some students used vile profanities; some professed hatred of other teachers; and some recalled sexual exploits and experience with the use of controlled substances. In each case, Rodney made no judgments and respected what he saw as the private thoughts of the writer.

As Rodney worked his way to the bottom of the stack of writer's logs, he opened one log that he found particularly disturbing. The log belonged to Kyle Pattard, a reserved but generally cooperative 11th-grade student. Kyle's log entry was apparently a response to a recent class discussion about persuasion and policy issues. The example that the class explored was the government interdiction with regard to refugees who had attempted to reach the United States by boat from Haiti and Cuba. The following is what Kyle wrote:

> Drown the boat people! We don't need one more Cuban in this country. Their attempts to reach America by boat should be considered an invasion. The navy and the coast guard should blow them out of the water. Put me on a gunboat. I'll be happy to pull the trigger. Here's my policy: death to the beaners!

On the top of the page, Kyle had printed in large letters "KILL, KILL, KILL!" He also illustrated his entry by drawing a crude picture of a boat in flames and a gunner laughing at the destruction (see Figure 3A, "Writer's Log Entry").

Of course, Rodney was stunned and disgusted when he came across this entry. His instinctive reaction was to write a long, critical response to Kyle, pointing out his failure to use reason and urging him to abandon the hateful attitude represented by the log entry. Rodney hesitated to write, and he reflected on the potential seriousness of Kyle's comments.

Any threats of physical violence in schools would have to be taken seriously. In the past year in the same state, there had been three cases of shootings in schools. During the fall semester, there was a bomb threat in a neighboring district, where police specialists had had to remove a homemade pipe bomb from the girls' locker room. In each case, the perpetrator was a disaffected student who expressed rage against a target group in the school.

As Rodney reflected on the log entry, a representative image of Kyle Pattard came to mind. Rodney could picture Kyle in camouflage fatigue pants, black t-shirt, and combat boots. He sported a close-cropped haircut. A chain connected Kyle's wallet to his military-style belt. Rodney did not want to stereotype Kyle, but he couldn't help but think of Kyle as fitting the image of a member of a militia group.

FIGURE 3A

Writer's Log Entry

KILL , KILL , KILL!

Drown the boat people! We don't need one more Cuban in this country. Their attempts to reach America by boat should be considered an invasion. The navy and the coast guard should blow them out of the water. Put me on a gunboat. I'll be happy to pull the trigger. Here's my policy: death to the beaners!

Kyle's writer's log entry triggered memories of some unfortunate episodes in class. Rodney recalled that Kyle commonly avoided the Latino students in class. Whenever there was cooperative group work, Kyle discreetly asked not to be teamed with Latino students. Rodney, of course, refused such requests, recognizing that a strength of cooperative learning is that students learn how to work with everyone. However, when Kyle was teamed with Latino students, he remained silent, sitting with arms folded, contributing nothing to the group. Since Latino students comprised approximately 30% of the school population, it was inevitable that most cooperative groups would include at least one Latino student.

As Rodney read and reread Kyle's writer's log entry, he wondered how serious the threat was. He feared that there was an immediate concern because a significant portion of the school's enrollment was Latino, most of whom were Cuban American. Rodney feared that Kyle may be capable of a violent attack or that an overt expression of his hate-ful attitude might prompt a violent response. At the same time, none of Kyle's other writer's log entries had the same tone or expressed similar sentiments. Rodney wondered if perhaps he was overreacting.

Rodney knew that, if the log entry even hinted at a child's suicidal tendencies or if the entry expressed an overt threat to a particular student or teacher, he would have to share the student's writing with some authorities who could intervene. In this case, how-ever, Rodney wondered that, although he was disgusted with the ideas Kyle expressed, he could not judge that Kyle posed a genuine threat.

Rather than ponder the question alone, Rodney decided to phone Yolanda Beekers, a veteran science teacher whom the school district had assigned to him as a mentor. When Rodney reached her, Yolanda observed, "Maybe the boy is just trying to shock you. If he has not gotten into trouble before and hasn't posed a real threat in your class, maybe he is just exaggerating, the way adolescent boys will. I would talk to him, though; and I would show the writing to the assistant principal. I know you want to keep the writing confidential, but you also have to protect yourself."

Yolanda was definite about what she thought Rodney should do, but he still felt un-comfortable about sharing the student's writing after promising that he would keep the logs confidential. In a way, Rodney felt that he would violate a promise and contradict the approach he was trying to take in the teaching of writing.

Rodney Welkins faces at least two major decisions: (1) What, if anything, should he write as a response in Kyle's log or say to Kyle in a conference? (2) Should Rodney vio-late the promise of confidentiality and share Kyle's writer's log entry with other adults in school or with Kyle's parents, without Kyle's permission? **If you were in Rodney's situation, what would you do?**

QUESTIONS FOR DISCUSSION

1. What are the possible courses of action Rodney might take? For each possible course of action, identify the likely benefits and potential disadvantages.
2. In this case, is Rodney obliged to keep his pledge to confidentiality? Explain.
3. According to the information presented in this case, is Rodney under any legal obligations to report Kyle's written views to anyone?
4. In this case, does Kyle have a right to the privacy of his thoughts? Explain.
5. Should Rodney in this situation have a compelling concern for the safety and dignity of Kyle's classmates? Why or why not?
6. Does Rodney have a right and a responsibility to try to change Kyle's views? Explain.
7. Is it possible and practical for any teacher to make the kind of pledge of confidentiality that Rodney has made with his students? Why or why not?
8. Part of Rodney's dilemma stems from his approach to the teaching of writing. Comment on the merits of his approach and the assumptions he makes about how students develop as writers.

9. Identify short-term and long-term solutions to the problem. Be prepared to explain your plan in detail.

RELATED RESEARCH AND WRITING

Research *one* of the following topics, prepare a written report, and share your findings with your colleagues.

1. Read the work of someone who is a proponent of using journal writing and "free writing" as a means to develop writing skills and to discover an authentic voice for writing. See, for example, the work of Ken Macrorie. Why does the proponent find it important for writers to use journals? What problems might a teacher face when he or she relies on journal writing as an essential part of writing instruction?

2. Talk to personnel who have the responsibility for security at a local school. To what extent do they judge their school to be a safe environment? What are their primary security concerns? What are they doing to provide a reasonable guarantee of safety in the school? To what extent must a teacher be concerned about safety?

3. Read reports about the current state of safety and security in schools. How have schools changed in regard to security in the past 10 years? Generally, have schools become safer places for children? Have schools been doing more to protect the safety of children?

4. Talk to a teacher in a local school. Find out what teachers are *required* to do when they read in students' writing some issues about neglect, abuse, the potential for violent behavior, and the suggestion of suicide. What guidelines do teachers have for determining when a student is making a veiled threat or when the student is crying out for help? Report to your classmates or colleagues about what you learned about the local policies.

5. Laws regarding the disclosure of students' writing to parents, school officials, and other authorities differ from state to state. For example, in some states, such as Illinois, the law requires that, if teachers obtain information about possible child abuse or neglect from students' writing, then they must report that information to the proper authorities. Investigate the laws in your state regarding the kind of information and under what circumstances teachers are required to disclose to parents, school officials, or other authorities the information they learn from students' writing. How do the laws in your state relate to the kind of problem presented in this case?

4 The Accu-grade System: What Is a Fair Grade?

PREVIEW

Teachers commonly complain that grading is one of the worst aspects of their jobs. Not only is the task tedious, but the teacher inevitably faces some difficult and emotional decisions. As much as teachers try to make grading as objective and accurate as possible with the use of computer gradebook programs, some judgment calls will be necessary. In the following case, the teacher faces several awkward judgment calls. He knows that the numbers in his gradebook do not add up to his impressions of the students' capabilities. The teacher is left to ponder how to be fair to all of his students.

FOCUS QUESTIONS

As you read the case, keep the following questions in mind: (1) How would you grade the four students who are profiled? (2) How can the teacher determine a reasonable and fair grade for each student? (3) How can the teacher be fair and consistent at the same time?

THE CASE

The Accu-grade System: What Is a Fair Grade?

Jeremy Flanders dreaded making decisions about students' grades at the end of the semester. As he pondered his gradebook on this late evening in January, he faced the kind of assessment anomalies that seriously disturbed him. Jeremy had been using a gradebook program on his home computer to record and calculate grades. Jeremy had hoped that the gradebook software would make his decisions easier and more objective: Just enter the credit for tests and assignments and the computer calculates the grade. Jeremy could provide each student with a printout and say, "There you have it. The numbers don't lie." But Jeremy was discovering that there were some inevitable subjective judgments he must make without the assistance of the computer. The difficulty in making decisions about grades was apparent in the case of four of Jeremy's students. These students were in Jeremy's "average ability" sophomore English class. Their computer-generated grade profiles appear below.

Accu-grade
Summary Grade Report
Teacher: Flanders

Whitney Patel

Homework Assign	Tests/ Quizzes	Major Essays	Semester Exam	Semester Total	Semester Percent
200	225	140	75	640	75.3
200	350	200	170	850	100

Stephania Radzienski

Homework Assign	Tests/ Quizzes	Major Essays	Semester Exam	Semester Total	Semester Percent
200	50	112	106	468	55
200	350	200	170	850	100

Jamal Wicker

Homework Assign	Tests/ Quizzes	Major Essays	Semester Exam	Semester Total	Semester Percent
25	90	185	165	465	54.7
200	350	200	170	850	100

Axel Wiscomb

Homework Assign	Tests/ Quizzes	Major Essays	Semester Exam	Semester Total	Semester Percent
170	200	125	85	580	68
200	350	200	170	850	100

The four profiles were puzzling. First, there was Whitney Patel. An examination of the numbers would indicate that she passes with a *C*, at 75.3%. Whitney is a student who attends class regularly and completes all her assignments. She passes mostly on the strength of her homework completion. She has also done reasonably well on the assignments that Jeremy has labeled "major essays," which means multiple-paragraph compositions that had been developed through a deliberate process over several days. For Jeremy, the troubling aspect of the grade profile was the fact that Whitney performed very poorly on the semester exam (44%). The semester exam requires that students answer comprehension questions about the short texts that they read on the day of the test and that they write an essay. Presumably, the semester exam provides a measure of how well students can *independently* read and write. One would have to wonder, then, how it is possible to pass Whitney if she cannot demonstrate that she can read and write at a level of performance that is expected of 10th-graders. Although Whitney completed all of her homework assignments, and she earned fairly good grades on her essays, these sources of assessment did not provide measures of independent work. In fact, sometimes Jeremy wondered if Whitney's parents had actually done most of her work for her. In the end, the only thing that Jeremy could say with certainty was that

Whitney Patel is a conscientious student who attends class every day and completes all of her homework. Jeremy could not say that Whitney could read and write the way students are expected to in 10th grade. Jeremy thought, "If I pass Whitney, it is basically because she is a nice kid who does all her work, and the computer tells me that I have a numerical basis for passing her."

Stephania posed another kind of problem. The numbers would indicate that she should fail the class at 55 percent. Jeremy had already followed the school policy by notifying parents when students were failing or near failing, so a failing grade would come as no surprise to any of his students having difficulties. Like Whitney, Stephania completed all of her homework, but she performed poorly on tests and quizzes. Many of the quizzes were basic recall questions, which were intended to prompt the students to keep up with their assigned reading. Stephania also had some difficulty with the major essays. At the same time, on the semester exam, a measure of students' independent ability to read and write, Stephania earned a passing grade. In the end, Jeremy wondered, didn't the semester exam in itself show that this student achieved the goals of the course? The problem was further complicated because Jeremy knew that Stephania had Tourette's syndrome and was legally blind in one eye. Perhaps her ability to overcome these challenges makes her performance on the semester exam even stronger. But shouldn't she be held to the same performance standards as all the other students in 10th grade?

If Jeremy felt uncomfortable in failing Stephania, he felt even worse about the prospect of passing Axel Wiscomb. Like Whitney, Axel had difficulty with the semester exam. In fact, he failed miserably, with a 50% score. If one relied on the semester exam alone, Jeremy would have to say that Axel cannot read or write at the standard that could reasonably be expected of 10th graders. Consistently, Axel's essay grades were Ds. He barely scraped by on essays and tests when he was provided a lot of support in class. When he worked independently, he could not make a passing grade. Although he would not openly admit it, Jeremy thought he would *like* to fail Axel. His attendance was irregular, and he was often tardy for class. Axel was often disruptive in class and occasionally disrespectful toward Jeremy. In general, Jeremy thought that Axel had a "bad attitude," yet his grade was close to a *C*, according to Jeremy's scale. In fact, if he were a more pleasant and cooperative student, Jeremy would be tempted to round the score off to an even 70%. But Jeremy wanted to remain objective.

Perhaps the most distressing situation of all was Jamal's. His total score and percentage (54.7%) for the semester would indicate that he should fail. In fact, the total percentage revealed that he is not close to passing. There isn't even the possibility to round the final percentage in his favor. He has turned in almost no homework, and he has little accumulated credit on tests and quizzes because he has been absent frequently and has never made up the tests that he has missed. At the same time, he has done remarkably well on the major essays. In fact, Jeremy remembers showing one of his colleagues Jamal's essay about *Dr. Jeckyl and Mr. Hyde,* and they both agreed that the essay was brilliant. Jeremy knew that Jamal had written the essays himself, because Jeremy had seen the early drafts of the essays as the students worked on them in class. Jeremy was confident that Jamal's essays were reliable evidence of his considerable writing ability.

Jeremy had a lot of sympathy for Jamal. His father died when Jamal was very young. Now his mother is battling cancer, for which she receives regularly scheduled chemotherapy. The chemo treatment leaves Ms. Wicker weak and incapacitated. At these times, Jeremy takes over responsibilities at home, causing him to be absent frequently.

There are several emotional reasons for Jeremy to recognize mitigating circumstances and pass Jamal. To complicate matters, Jamal is a high scoring forward on the school's boys varsity basketball team. Jamal's failure might make him ineligible to play, which would have a devastating impact on the team and would deny Jamal one motivation for staying in school during a trying period in the Wicker family's life. At the same time, Jeremy had always carefully avoided showing favoritism toward star athletes. If Jeremy were to pass Jamal at 55%, he might as well pass everyone in the class.

Jeremy recalled that his principal, Dr. Flores, emphasized that he should call her at any time if he had a question about anything. He knew it would help to talk about his questions with someone more experienced, but he worried that it was too late to call and he doubted that he had Dr. Flores' home number, anyway.

As Jeremy pondered his dilemma, he reminded himself that the goals for English focus on *literacy*, not on regular *attendance* or the *amount* of homework completed. Jeremy also told himself that he has a responsibility to the students and to his colleagues to be consistent, or else any assessment would be meaningless. As difficult as it was going to be, Jeremy would have to make decisions and turn in grades the next day. **What grades should he submit for these four students? How can he justify his decisions?**

QUESTIONS FOR DISCUSSION

1. On what factors should Jeremy base his decisions about the grades for the four students? Is it possible to be absolutely objective? If one is justified in making some subjective judgments, where does that subjectivity end?
2. What are the dangers in making subjective, or even impressionistic, judgments in regard to the assessment of students' academic performance?
3. Presumably, Jeremy will leave printed documentation of his grades with the school's central office. Is there any real danger that someone would question him if he were to pass a student when the numbers in the gradebook don't seem to support the grade?
4. Jeremy is in danger of letting emotion and sentiment influence his judgments about students' grades. To what extent do these *feelings* have an appropriate place in assigning grades?
5. To what extent should Jeremy take into account the potential reactions of his colleagues to any decision he makes about grades for his own students?
6. What do you think about Jeremy's *system* of grading? Are there any adjustments he might make to allow the system to support the grades that he is inclined to make anyway? In a sense, would this adjustment be stacking the deck against some students and in favor of others? Explain.
7. How can Jeremy assign grades that will be consistent with his inclinations and allow him to justify his decisions as fair and accurate?

RELATED RESEARCH AND WRITING

Research *one* of the following topics, prepare a written report, and share your findings with your colleagues.

1. Work with at least two computer-based grade programs. What assumptions do the software producers appear to make about student learning and assessment? What are the strengths of each program? What cautions would you offer someone who will rely on such software?

2. Talk to at least two veteran teachers about the system that they use for grading. After your conversation, devise your own system. Describe your system to your classmates or colleagues and provide the rationale for grading the way you propose to do.

5 *Teaching for the Test*

PREVIEW

Although teachers typically enjoy a great deal of autonomy in their own classrooms, no teacher has complete freedom. Various sources impose demands on the teacher. A beginning teacher will feel pressure to conform, even when conformity means compromising the instructional approaches that appear to have the greatest merit. How can the teacher maintain instructional integrity and answer the demands of others? Is it realistic for a teacher to expect to teach the way he or she was trained to teach as a student in a methods class?

FOCUS QUESTIONS

As you read the following case, prepare to discuss these questions: (1) Must the teacher in this case follow an instructional plan that the school principal sponsors? How much autonomy does the teacher have to make the instructional decisions in her own classroom? (2) To what extent should the mandated state assessments guide a teacher's instructional plans?

THE CASE

Teaching for the Test

When Esmeralda Huerta went to her faculty mailbox during the first week of February, she found a note from the principal's secretary: "Please stop by the principal's office today to pick up your SAP material." Although Esmeralda was in her second year of teaching, it was her first for teaching sixth grade and her first experience in administering the state-mandated writing assessment. She viewed the test as an imposition on her instructional time, but she recognized that it was a requirement that all schools in her state were obliged to complete. Realistically, Esmeralda thought, she and her students could afford to sacrifice a couple of days of instruction in order to accommodate the writing test.

Esmeralda was surprised and more than a little annoyed when she picked up the test preparation materials and read the attached memo from the principal:

TO: Sixth-Grade Teachers
FROM: Eleanor Bobbins
DATE: January 27
SUBJECT: SAP Test Preparation

As I suggested at the beginning of the year, the six weeks before the State Assessment Program (SAP) tests will be devoted to preparing students to be successful on the exam. Remember that the students' performance on the tests is a reflection on our school and on your instruction. The attached booklets have been provided to assist you in preparing your students. You will follow the daily plan suggested in the booklets to train students for the exam. Please see me if you need more booklets or if you have any questions about their use.

When Esmeralda made her way to her classroom and examined some of the materials, she was crestfallen. In Esmeralda's judgment, the test preparation booklets that were intended for student use promoted formulaic writing and relied on simple-minded analogies. Essentially, the lessons in the booklet prompted students to use a rigid template to guide the production of compositions and structured practice with the state's scoring rubric for students to assess each other's papers.

One representative lesson directed students to conceive of the organization of their narrative as parts of a slice of pizza, with the supporting crust representing the overall focus and the toppings representing the descriptive details and expression of events (see Figure 5A). A graphic in the "SAP Lesson #3" suggests a numbered sequence for planning a narrative composition. The lessons for the persuasive writing sample encouraged the students to follow the "triangulation approach," which directs the writer to conceive of any topic as having three aspects or components. Under this system, the writer would express a general claim having three parts (see Figure 5B). For example, the writer might respond to a question about holding school on Saturdays by claiming in the introduction, "We should not have classes on Saturday because children need time to relax, teachers need time to prepare, and custodians need time to clean and repair the school building." In the body of the composition, the writer would develop each of these three reasons with supporting details and provide explicit and apparent transitions. In the conclusion, the writer would summarize the three reasons identified in the introduction and developed in the body of the paper.

Esmeralda judged that the lessons prescribed by the test preparation booklets were diametrically opposed to the kind of writing instruction she understood to be the most honest, effective, and worthwhile. The rigid and prescriptive nature of the lessons in the booklet would work against everything she tried to promote in creating a genuine literacy environment in her classroom. If she were to follow the lessons as defined in the test preparation booklets, she would be teaching in a way that ran counter to the practices that her university professor had sponsored in her methods classes.

As Esmeralda expressed her frustration in her discussions with other teachers, they offered a wide mixture of responses and advice. Bob Tewkes, a veteran of 23 years of teaching, observed, "What are you worried about? At least the students will get *some*

FIGURE 5A

SAP Lesson #3: Envisioning the Narrative Structure

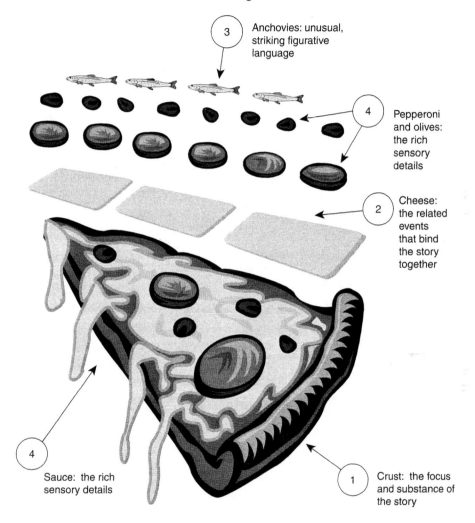

③ Anchovies: unusual, striking figurative language

④ Pepperoni and olives: the rich sensory details

② Cheese: the related events that bind the story together

④ Sauce: the rich sensory details

① Crust: the focus and substance of the story

instruction in writing. That's more than they got a few years ago. What harm is there? Someone has already planned your lessons for you. It's a good situation: the kids learn, and you have to work less."

Maria Wilson, another veteran teacher, insisted, "I'm not putting up with this nonsense. I have no intention of using the test preparation booklets and drilling students to become mindless automatons. Writing demands *thinking,* and I'm going to teach students to *think.* I'll pick up the booklets from the principal's office, but I'll dump them in the garbage. I'd like to see someone force me to teach students to write by following a formula!"

FIGURE 5B

SAP Lesson #6: The Triangulation Approach to Persuasive Writing

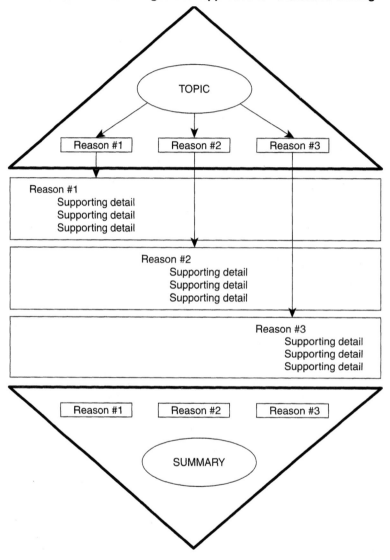

Zlada Dzimtra, another first-year teacher, reported, "I'm not a tenured teacher. I'm in no position to defy anyone. I want to keep my job, so I'll do as I'm told. I know that the test preparation material promotes practices that are opposed to the way that I was trained to teach writing, but I'll have to swallow my pride and do what is required."

Esmeralda understood the principal's concerns. The school had been on the state's "academic watch" list for the past two years. Ms. Bobbins was under a great deal of pressure to improve the scores on the state assessment. In fact, there was a possibility that Eleanor Bobbins would be replaced as principal if the school remained on the academic watch list.

It seemed to Esmeralda that, after teachers and students returned to school after the winter break, everything focused on the state exams. There were posters mounted in the halls and in classrooms to encourage students to demonstrate pride in the school by performing well on the tests. The principal sent home a letter to parents to suggest the appropriate regimen of diet and sleep to help children reach their optimum test-taking state. Ms. Bobbins scheduled a motivational speaker to meet with the students in an all-school assembly during the week before the tests. Esmeralda learned from veteran teachers that last year's motivational speaker not only described the importance of academic achievement but also led cheers to promote enthusiasm for taking the required tests. In addition, the PTA will provide free high-protein breakfasts at school on the days of the tests.

For the next 6 weeks, Esmeralda will be expected to follow the lessons in the test preparation materials. During that time, Esmeralda was sure to be observed by a supervisor. She resisted following the prescribed lessons, yet she felt the pressure to do what was required by the state and by the principal. **If you were Esmeralda what would you do? Should she accept Bob's advice and follow the safe route that Zlada was taking? Should she be defiant, like Maria, and remain true to her university training?**

QUESTIONS FOR DISCUSSION

1. Does Esmeralda have an obligation to teach the way that the principal prescribes and to allow her instruction to be guided by a state-mandated test? Why?
2. To what extent does Esmeralda have the academic freedom to design instruction that she judges to have the greatest educational value?
3. To what extent does each of Esmeralda's colleagues have a valid perspective and offer sound advice?
4. Could Esmeralda ignore the test preparation materials until a supervisor visits her classroom? If Esmeralda could circumvent the principal's directives, would this be advisable? Explain.
5. Should Esmeralda and her colleagues meet with the principal to discuss their concerns about the use of the test preparation booklets? What would be the likely result of such a meeting?

RELATED RESEARCH AND WRITING

Research *one* of the following topics, prepare a written report, and share your findings with your colleagues.

1. Investigate the pressures in a local school to have teachers conform to a prescribed curriculum or to focus instruction on preparation for mandated tests. Interview a principal or teacher in a grade that must participate in state-mandated tests. How does the principal or teacher feel about the expectation to conform to

the directives and standards that have been developed by people who might not be familiar with the school, its students, or its curriculum? To what extent does the individual teacher feel that he or she has the freedom to provide the instruction that the teacher deems best? To what extent does the principal or teacher feel that he or she is able to pursue the kind of instruction that seems to be the best in theory?

2. Interview teachers in a local school. To what extent do the teachers believe they have academic freedom? Does the school have an academic freedom committee? Does the school offer a written policy about academic freedom? What does the school do to safeguard academic freedom?

3. Read commentaries about mandated tests in your area. What arguments do supporters and detractors make about the mandated tests? Do the tests guide curriculum in a positive way? Do the tests provide important data about students? Do the tests allow schools to measure students' academic progress? Are the tests an important measure to hold schools and teachers accountable for quality instruction? Write your own position statement about the mandated tests, and share your position with classmates or colleagues.

6 It Can't Be This Difficult: Peer Revision Activities

PREVIEW

Any experienced English teacher will tell you that it is seldom easy to get students to think critically, particularly when it comes to being critical of their own writing or the writing of their peers. Students will often look for an easy way out, and if the opportunity is there they will usually take it. The teacher in the following case discovers just how difficult it can be to get her students to be critical of their own and their peers' writing. Despite the teacher's best efforts, her students continue to resist putting real effort into learning and practicing the revising and editing skills she wants them to learn. What can this teacher do to get her students to become serious about learning how to revise writing?

FOCUS QUESTIONS

As you read the following case, prepare to discuss these questions: (1) Why is this teacher having so much trouble trying to get her students to think critically about their own writing and the writing of others? To what extent does the teacher in this case contribute to her own problems? (2) What should the teacher do next to get her students to become more thoughtful and critical of their own writing and the writing of others? What long-term plan might she use to develop and reinforce the critical thinking and revision strategies she wants her students to learn and use whenever they write and revise their own writing or read and evaluate the writing of others?

THE CASE

It Can't Be This Difficult: Peer Revision Activities

Mary Goodheart was frustrated. Even though she was only a first year teacher, she felt that she was pretty strong when it came to the teaching of writing. She had attended a nearby state university, which was known for its strong teaching of writing program. When Mary was hired by Susan Lassiter, the principal of Abraham Lincoln Middle

School, Susan had said, "Look, Mary. I know you are inexperienced, but I'm hiring you because you seem to have some good ideas about how to teach writing, and I hope you'll be able to convince some of our senior teachers that there is more to teaching writing than memorizing grammar rules and drills. Heaven knows, I have tried, but I haven't made much progress. I'm assigning you to the eighth grade because that seems to be where we need the most work. Come and see me in a couple of months into the school year and let me know what you are doing and the progress you have made."

School had now been in session for almost 2 months, and Mary hadn't seen much progress at all. Mary hadn't anticipated how difficult it would be to get her students to be thoughtful about revising, especially when it came to being critical of their own or other students' writing. In her teacher education program, she had taken a course in the teaching of writing, where she and her classmates had spent a lot of time talking about the stages of the writing process and about peer revising and editing activities and why they are important. She had learned some peer evaluation and editing strategies, and the professor had even made them a part of what students in the class were expected to do with their own writing. However, Mary was learning that practicing some evaluation activities with a group of preservice teachers was very different from trying to do them with a group of middle school students.

What frustrated Mary most was that her students couldn't seem to comment constructively on their own or other students' writing. She had started by having her students meet in small groups to read and discuss compositions that they had written about a field trip to the zoo. She had had the students meet in small groups and had asked them to read their papers aloud one at a time, and then the groups were to make comments on the strengths and weaknesses of the papers. Unfortunately, after a few minutes most students were not on task, and it was clear that the group discussions focused more on social activities than the strengths and weaknesses of the students' writing. Mary tried to salvage the activity by refocusing it. After getting the groups quiet she said, "You seem to be having some trouble, so I want you to read each of the compositions aloud and then pick the best composition in the group. I'll come around to check on you and how you are doing. Does everyone understand what I want you to do?"

The refocused activity didn't go much better. One group would stay on task only if Mary stood right there with them. A second group quickly read through the papers and picked the one that was the longest because it had "a lot of details." A third group couldn't decide on the best composition and reported that they were all "really good." Another group picked the following composition as the best because, as Gary Ross, the spokesperson for his group, said, "It was short and to the point."

The Bayfed Zoo

I really liked the Bayfield zoo because it has alot of animals. My favorit is the mondkeys because they are funy. I also liked the snakes. The piethon was awesome. Next to it a ratlesnake who was sheding his skin. Another animail I like is the elefants, I saw them fed them some hay and carots and other vegatables. I think we shuld go too the bayfeld zoo every day for school.

When she asked the group about the grammar, spelling, and punctuation errors, Gary said, "We knew what the writer meant, so what's the big deal?"

"I'll tell you what the big deal is, young man!" Mary started to say a little too loudly, but then she took a deep breath and instead said, "Class, you don't see how important it is that you learn how to be critical of writing. You don't seem to see how important the revision stage of the writing process is, so we are going to have to do some more work on this."

Mary knew that her students needed some more guidance, but she wasn't sure exactly what to do. That night she met with Delores Smith, one of her friends from her teacher education program, who was teaching in a school district not far from Mary's middle school. Delores seemed very excited about the writing program at her high school. When Mary explained her problem, Delores said that she understood. Delores then explained that most of the teachers in her school used various kinds of evaluation sheets in their classes, some based on the state writing assessment, and they trained their students to use them. This approach offered promise in solving many of the problems Mary was talking about. In fact, part of each student's grade on some writing assignments was contingent on how well he or she evaluated other students' writing. Everyone in the department was convinced that this approach was effective, and there was some evidence that students' scores on the state writing assessment had gone up once the department started using the evaluation sheets.

Delores concluded her comments by saying, "I think the important thing is that the students are learning the criteria involved in producing effective writing, and they are applying those criteria when they evaluate their own or other students' writing." Delores gave one of the evaluation sheets to Mary (see Figure 6A). Mary had high hopes that this approach might help her with her problem.

The next morning, over coffee, Mary discussed her problem with Bill Worth, one of the other eighth-grade language arts teachers. After explaining what had happened in class, Mary summed it up this way: "They just wouldn't get serious about being critical of their own or one another's writing. I guess I sort of assumed that they had done peer evaluation before and I wouldn't need to tell them everything. Have you got any ideas about what I might try next?"

"I think you're right, Mary," Bill said. "They probably do need some more guidance. I like to do one or two compositions with them on the overhead and model for them what I want them to do when they evaluate a composition. I really believe in modeling strategies. I just happen to have one with me that I use for this very purpose. You are welcome to use it."

"Thanks, Bill. I really appreciate it."

Mary made up her mind what she was going to do. She made an overhead transparency of the composition, ran off a class set of the evaluation sheets, and then spent the next few minutes planning out her activity. When class started, she put the paper on the overhead projector (see Figure 6B), indicated that it had been written by an unnamed eighth-grade student in another class, and asked her students to read it and evaluate it using the evaluation sheet that she handed out. When she asked several students to read their comments, they ranged from overly critical to neutral to "It's very good; I like it." None of the comments was specific enough to the text to be useful to the writer, and far too many dealt with minor mechanical errors. One of her weakest spellers even managed to find four misspellings that were not in the paper. Another student's most

Descriptive Writing Evaluation Sheet

Evaluator's Name: _____

Author's Name: _____

Directions: Put a check next to the sentence that best describes how well the writer performs in each of the following five areas: focus, elaboration, dialogue, language, and mechanics.

I. Focus

_____ Clear and sharp with strong impact—details all work to create an overall impression

_____ Sometimes marred by material that is irrelevant or that does not contribute to the central impression

_____ Tends to jump from one idea to another—does not create an overall impression

II. Elaboration

_____ Good use of specific, concrete detail

_____ Includes a variety of sensory imagery

_____ Uses some effective figurative language (simile, metaphor, personification, etc.)

_____ Uses some specific, concrete detail but needs to include more

_____ Includes some descriptions that are clichéd (overused and unoriginal)

_____ Includes very little specific, concrete detail

_____ Includes many clichés

_____ Needs to include more variety of sensory imagery (sound, touch, taste, smell)

_____ Needs to include more figurative language (simile, metaphor, personification, etc.)

III. Dialogue (if applicable)

_____ Effective use of direct dialogue

_____ Some effective use of direct dialogue

_____ Needs to use direct dialogue more often when people are conversing

_____ Needs to use direct dialogue when people are conversing

IV. Language

_____ Effective word choice ("The child lazily waddled down the street")

_____ Satisfactory word choice ("The child lazily walked down the street")

_____ Weak word choice ("The child went down the street")

V. Mechanics, usage, spelling, etc.

_____ Good

_____ Satisfactory

_____ Weak

Grade I would give the composition: _____

FIGURE 6B

MODEL STUDENT COMPOSITION

Second Floor LRC

As I sit here trying to think of a topic to write, I can hear the sounds of whispering people behind me. I look up and I can see many colors of cloths with people, whom I havent met, in them. Now someone clumpes along the floor, then that same person whirls the pencil sharpenor over the pencil. Satisfied, he walks away. I hear the teacher mumbling something about divisin as he helps someone with a math problem. I hear a jingle and I turn around to see the janiter behind me picking papers as he goes along. Someone giggles and I stop thinking for a minute. The buzing sound of the lights above is bugging me. Now I hear the sound, somewhat like a zipper, of someone tearing a sheet of pape from their spiral notebook. The hum of the bell reminds me I must leave. I have to go to my next class, I rush down the stairs and study period is over.

---

helpful comment was, "It's dumb!" Mary concluded that her students were obviously not yet ready to be turned loose evaluating their own or others' papers.

As Mary left the classroom that day, she wondered what had gone wrong. Had she provided too much guidance or structure? Had she overwhelmed the students with too many things to consider? Perhaps they hadn't worked enough with descriptive writing to understand what was meant by "specific details," "figurative language," or some of the other terminology. Maybe she just hadn't pushed them enough to explain and defend their responses. Maybe these students weren't mature enough to handle being critical of writing. She wondered if her students would ever learn to be critical of their own and others' writing. **What else could she do? If you were in Mary's situation, what would you do?**

QUESTIONS FOR DISCUSSION

1. What is the best explanation for why Mary is having so much trouble getting her students to learn how to be critical of their own and their peers' writing?
2. To what extent does Mary contribute to the problems her students are having? In other words, what mistakes does she make? How could she correct some mistakes?
3. Mary starts to let Gary Ross really have it when he makes what seems to be a smart remark about grammar, spelling, and punctuation, but then she backs off and makes a general comment to the class. Was this the right strategy? Why or why not?
4. What would you have done differently the day Mary used the overhead and handout of the criteria? Why? If you were Bill or Delores and Mary approached you about what happened in class that day, what would you say to her? Why?
5. Clearly, Mary's beliefs about teaching writing were shaped by her teacher education program. To what extent is her teacher education program responsible for the problems she is having? Do teacher education programs have a

responsibility to follow up and provide help for their graduates once they become teachers? Why or why not?

6. If Susan Lassiter, the principal, asks Mary how she is doing with the writing program, what should she say? Why? Is it likely that the principal will be critical of Mary's performance? Why or why not?

7. Do you think that the principal has a responsibility to help Mary with her situation? Why or why not? To what extent do you think the principal will be willing and able to help Mary? Do you think the principal was asking too much of Mary in this situation? Why or why not?

8. What short-term and long-term solutions can you devise for Mary? What is the best course of action for her to take? Why?

9. One major difference between Mary's and Delores' situations is that at Delores' school there seems to be a departmentwide writing program that includes a significant emphasis on revising and editing writing. How important is it that an English department or schoolwide writing program place a high priority on holding students accountable for revising and editing their own writing?

RELATED RESEARCH AND WRITING

Select *one* of the following areas of investigation, research the topic, and produce a brief written report that you can share with your colleagues.

1. Read a book such as Nancy Atwell's (1998) *In the Middle: New Understandings About Writing, Reading, and Learning* (2nd ed.) (Portsmouth, NH: Boynton/Cook) or George Hillocks, Jr.'s (1995) *Teaching Writing as Reflective Practice* (New York, NY: Teachers College Press) that discusses strategies for engaging students in the writing process and learning how to write and revise writing. What are the strengths and weaknesses of this approach? Do you think the approach would be effective with students? Why or why not?

2. Talk to an experienced middle school or high school English teacher about problems he or she has had with getting students to be critical of their own and others' writing. What are the major problem areas? Why? How did he or she address these problems?

3. Examine a few articles out of journals, such as *English Journal, Voices from the Middle, Classroom Notes Plus,* or *The Clearing House,* that suggest various approaches or strategies for dealing with revising and editing writing. What are some of the most promising approaches or strategies? Why? How do these methods get students to be thoughtful about or critical of their own and others' writing?

7 Out of Control: Delinquent or Disabled?

PREVIEW

Occasionally, a teacher will experience a class or a particular student who poses significant challenges for the orderly management of students and instruction. The teacher ponders why students are disruptive and uncooperative and struggles to figure out how to correct unruly behavior. In the following case, a teacher feels some dread about meeting with her class and worries about the options available to her to correct a bad situation. She will have to draw on what she knows about the psychology of adolescents and invoke whatever help and resources are available within the school.

FOCUS QUESTIONS

As you read the following case, keep these questions in mind: (1) Does the teacher face a significant problem? How do you know whether the problem is serious or superficial? (2) Why has the problem occurred? (3) What can the teacher do so that she finds her class productive and no longer dreads each class meeting?

THE CASE
Out of Control: Delinquent or Disabled?

Although it was a cool October morning and the faculty workroom was a chilly 58 degrees, Karen Moskovitz could feel perspiration build on her forehead and upper lip. She was almost physically ill contemplating the prospect of facing her unruly third-period sophomore English class. It seemed that several forces combined to make the third period the worst possible learning environment.

The class met in the late morning, when the adolescents were beginning to wake up and become lively. The students had not yet gone to lunch, so they were usually hungry. The class included several students with various learning challenges. In fact, it seemed that everyone in class had some sort of significant learning challenge. There were five students with active Individualized Educational Plans (IEPs). Four other students had been identified as attention deficit disordered (ADD) or attention deficit/hyperactivity disordered (ADHD). These students had their own accommodation plans. Two other students were in the school's Title 1 reading program, which means that they had significant difficulty with reading and a pronounced reluctance to read. Three other students were making a transition from English as a Second Language (ESL) classes to a mainstream English class. Since English was their second language, they lacked confidence and struggled to follow directions and complete assignments. One student was a recent immigrant from Lithuania. Although he knew little English, his parents insisted that he participate in a mainstream English class rather than an ESL class.

With all these learning challenges and the plans and accommodations that other school personnel had written for the students, Karen was overwhelmed by the multiple details and interventions she was supposed to attend to. And every day it seemed that the students were wound up on caffeine. They couldn't sit still in their seats, they said aloud whatever was on their minds whenever they wanted, and they seldom paid attention to directions. Karen could not rely on the students to complete homework or to bring the appropriate materials to class. Frequently, Karen found herself shouting above the general din of the class in an attempt to achieve some order. After third period on most days, Karen felt completely worn out and defeated.

The most disturbing element of the class was a student named Darnell Holloway. Although there was no accommodation plan for Darnell, his counselor reported that the family physician had diagnosed him as ADHD and had prescribed regular doses of Ritalin. Karen found Darnell completely incorrigible. During every class meeting, Karen repeatedly corrected Darnell for turning around in his desk and disturbing the student behind him. Karen would have moved him to a seat where he would be away from distractions, but every location in the classroom seemed to pose a distraction. He compulsively talked out of turn, with comments that had little or no relevance to the focus of the lesson. If he felt like talking to someone across the room, he simply shouted above any other discussion. If he felt like looking out the window, tossing something in the wastebasket, or sharpening a pencil, he immediately followed his impulses. Karen corrected Darnell repeatedly, but he appeared oblivious to attempts at controlling his behavior. Karen decided that part of his problem was the fact that his regular dose of Ritalin did not occur until after her class.

Lately, Darnell has become more and more belligerent to Karen's attempts to correct his behavior. If she makes simple requests, such as directing him to take out his book, he argues with her. Darnell's responses have taken this form: "Why do I need to take out the book? I'm not going to read it, anyway. It's a stupid book." If Karen directs Darnell to stop talking or turning around, he responds, "Why are you always picking on me? You don't say anything to anyone else."

Karen has talked to Darnell's mother several times. She seems sympathetic but reports that Darnell's behavior is connected to a physical disorder that she is trying to control with medication. Darrell's mother seems to be at a loss to change his behavior. Karen has given Darnell detentions, but he usually doesn't show up. She has sent him to the dean on a discipline referral, but the dean has done little more than scold Darnell and send him back to class. After Darnell missed three opportunities to serve a detention, the dean gave him a one-day in-school suspension. The dean told Karen, "There's not much I can do. His hyperactivity is his disability. I can't very well punish him for a behavioral disability any more than I can punish a student for having a physical disability."

There were two aspects of Darnell's behavior that she found particularly disturbing at this point. She knew that his behavior was a distraction to the rest of the class. This was apparent because, when Darnell was absent, the class had a much more purposeful, orderly, and cooperative atmosphere. It was clear that he had a negative impact on the learning of all the students. Second, Karen feared that Darnell's responses to her and to his classmates would become more and more volatile. She has yet to witness any violent behavior from Darnell, but she sensed that he was capable of becoming violent if provoked. And it was hard to predict what Darnell might find provocative.

Karen has followed the usual course of interventions. She corrected Darnell in class; she spoke to him outside of class about his behavior; she assigned detentions; she spoke to the parent; and she referred the student to the dean. Karen felt that she had run out of options. Although Karen felt that she had taken all the reasonable courses of action in an effort to manage her class, she worried that, if her supervisor were to observe the class, she would judge Karen as a weak teacher who had allowed the class to run out of control. At the end of her planning period, Karen would face Darnell and the rest of her very challenging third-period class. There was bound to be trouble. **How should she respond when Darnell acts up again today? What long-term intervention can she put in place to help Darnell and the rest of the class for the balance of the school year?**

QUESTIONS FOR DISCUSSION

1. Why does Darnell act the way he does? Is it possible for him to control his behavior, or for his behavior to be controlled?
2. Explain whether or not Karen has exhausted all the means available to her to manage her class. What else, if anything, could Karen have done? Would any other action on her part have had a different effect?
3. What can Karen do immediately to bring her unruly class under control and avoid an ugly confrontation?
4. Could Karen solicit the aid of any other school personnel—the nurse, a counselor, her supervisor, or another teacher? What help could any of these other persons provide? Would there be any negative consequences for inviting help from others?
5. To what extent would it be useful for Karen to seek to have Darnell removed from her class? Is his removal a realistic possibility? What would be the disadvantages, if any, to removing Darnell?
6. Devise a long-term plan for Karen to help her create a more orderly and productive atmosphere in her class and to help her cope with a very stressful situation. Who would be involved with this plan? What actions should she take? What makes you think any new measures would help?

RELATED RESEARCH AND WRITING

Research *one* of the following topics, prepare a written report, and share your findings with your colleagues.

1. Write your own case study to describe a troublesome student or disruptive class that you have witnessed during the thousands of hours you have spent in schools. What was done to try to correct the situation? What efforts were helpful? What efforts seemed to have little positive effect?

2. Interview an experienced teacher about a class or a student who posed considerable management problems for him or her. In writing, recount the situation for your colleagues. What interventions did the teacher try? What worked? What did not work? How does the teacher account for the relative efficaciousness of the actions?

3. Read about children who are labeled *behavioral disordered*. How is this condition defined? What are the signs or symptoms that would allow someone to identify a student as behavioral disordered? If the student has been identified as having such a disability, to what extent must a teacher treat his or her classroom behavioral issues differently?

8 It's Just a Soccer Game: How Will These Students View Me?

PREVIEW

A common challenge for any teacher is the defining of the relationship between the teacher and the students. Some young teachers are fairly close in age to high school seniors, which in a way invites a casual familiarity. In their roles as coaches and club advisors, teachers meet students under more relaxed conditions, and there is a natural inclination to develop a friendly rapport. More experienced teachers also cannot help but develop a fondness and closeness with students. In the following case, a young teacher must decide when a close relationship with students might become an impediment to his role as teacher. He must determine if it would be best for him to distance himself from students, even at the risk of being thought of as stuffy and too conservative.

FOCUS QUESTIONS

As you study the following case, consider these questions: (1) Is Brandon Shaker in a dangerous situation? What, if anything, does he have to worry about? (2) Should Brandon investigate anything before he acts? What, if anything, would he investigate? How would he proceed? (3) What should be Brandon's immediate course of action? Does he need to devise a policy for the future? If he does, what would it be?

THE CASE

It's Just a Soccer Game: How Will These Students View Me?

Brandon Shaker had been looking forward to this Saturday afternoon. Brandon was an enthusiastic soccer fan. He enjoyed soccer in many ways—as a player, as a coach, and as a spectator. At Gompers East, a suburban high school where Brandon taught English, his soccer enthusiasm and experience landed him the job as girls varsity soccer coach. On this particular weekend, Brandon had invited two of his close friends to his apartment in the city to watch on large screen television the delayed telecast of Tottenham Hotspur and Manchester United, two of the top teams in the English Premier League.

Brandon's friends, Jason Striker and Chase Medfield, both in their early 20s, remained at the apartment while Brandon ran to the store for more beer and snacks. All the pieces were falling into place for a great afternoon of soccer viewing.

When Brandon returned with bags of beer, tortilla chips, and pork rinds, there was no place to park in front of the building, and he was forced to double-park as he unloaded. After Brandon climbed the stairs and opened the door to his apartment, he was met with a surprise. Leslie Ducati and Wendy Burgher, two senior members of the Gompers East varsity girls soccer team, were sitting in Brandon's living room with his two friends. As Brandon stepped into the room, it appeared to him that he interrupted an animated conversation between his friends and the girls. One look at Jason and Chase told Brandon that his friends were delighted with the company of the two girls, who, dressed in athletic shorts and tank tops, would easily appear to be mature college students. "Surprised to see us, Mr. Shaker?" asked Leslie.

"You *could* say that," replied Brandon, as he nearly dropped a bag of beer on the floor.

"We've been enjoying the company of these two lovely ladies," said Jason.

"What are you doing here?" Brandon asked the girls.

"We came to watch the game with the world's biggest soccer fan," said Wendy.

Anticipating Brandon's response, Leslie said, "Don't make us go, Mr. Shaker. I called my dad and he said we could stay. We're just going to watch the game and then we're on our way."

"Come on, Mr. Shaker," said Wendy. "Don't be a killjoy, Mr. S.! You're the only one we know who has the cable television service that shows today's match. And you've got this big screen television! Come on, Mr. S."

"You're not making us leave now, Mr. S., not after we drove all the way into the city," Leslie insisted.

"We'll see," said Brandon. He put the beer and snacks in the kitchen and made his way downstairs to move his car. As Brandon went to his car, he had a little time to ponder this awkward situation and there *was* a lot to think about.

Leslie's words echoed in Brandon's head: "Don't be a killjoy, Mr. S.!" In his first 2 years of teaching at Gompers East, he had developed a very strong rapport with the students. In general, he felt that the students liked him—the students in his classes, the students on his soccer team, even students he didn't know. There were several reasons for the rapport: He was one of the younger teachers in the school, he could talk to students candidly about the things that interested them, and he avoided being severely judgmental. Brandon remembered one student's assessment on his course evaluation: "You are awesome, Mr. S. You are not uptight like the other teachers."

As Brandon got into his car, he wondered if there was any possible way that he could allow the girls to stay. If the girls did indeed call their parents and got permission, there could be nothing to worry about. But Brandon hadn't actually talked to the parents himself. He wondered, "Could I call them myself and get the permission from each parent over the phone?" One complication was that Leslie's parents were separated. Could he accept permission from just one parent?

If Brandon insisted that the girls go, he knew that from that moment forward he would be "bogus." In the minds of his team and in the minds of most of his students, he would have joined the ranks of the conservative veteran teachers, separating himself from the lives of his students and refusing to take chances. If he didn't allow the girls to stay, how would he actually manage to rid himself of them? Leslie would be difficult. She was liable to hold onto a sofa leg and dare him to drag her away!

As he slowly circled the block, Brandon pulled his cell phone out of the glove compartment and phoned his Aunt Honora, who had taught elementary school for 30 years. When he described the situation to her, Aunt Honora did not hesitate: "Get those girls out of there right now, Brandon. You are just looking for trouble. Those girls may be perfectly naïve and innocent, but I don't know that your friends are. You've got to think about the impression their presence is going to make on people who learn about their visit." Brandon knew his aunt was right, but he had to figure out what, precisely, he was going to do.

Brandon pulled his car into an open parking space at the end of the block and exited the car. As he paced down the street, he remembered his friends' eagerness to have the girls stay to watch the soccer match. To them, they were just two attractive young women, not school girls. It seemed perfectly natural to have them stay to enjoy the match.

Brandon ascended the stairs to his apartment and wondered, "When I open that door, what am I going to do?" **If you were in Brandon's position, what would *you* do?**

QUESTIONS FOR DISCUSSION

1. Brandon is concerned about the presence of the students. What is the basis for his concern? Is his concern needless? Explain.
2. If Brandon wished to find answers to resolve some of the doubts he has, how would he proceed?
3. Should Brandon be concerned about the opinions and feelings of his students if he insists that his unexpected visitors leave? How will his decision affect the rapport he has with his students in the future?
4. If the two students resist leaving the apartment, how can Brandon influence them to depart?
5. If the two girls have their parents' permission to stay, should Brandon let them? Explain.
6. When Brandon returns to his apartment, what should he do? What factors influenced your recommendation?

RELATED RESEARCH AND WRITING

Research *one* of the following topics, prepare a written report, and share your findings with your colleagues.

1. Discuss with someone at a local school the policy that should guide a teacher's behavior in regard to contacts with students outside of class. For example, are teachers cautioned not to give students rides home after practice or after other extracurricular events? Are teachers advised not to meet with students outside of

class time? If teachers do have conferences with students outside of class, what precautions do the teachers take?

2. Interview a young teacher about any difficulty he or she has had in balancing a teacher *persona* and a friend *persona* in dealing with some friendly and likeable students. What challenges has the teacher experienced? To what extent have the difficulties been the product of the teacher's relative youth? How has the teacher managed to maintain a balance without compromising his or her integrity?

3. Recall any close relationships you have had with teachers or coaches. Have there ever been times when you sensed the teacher trying to maintain some personal distance? Have there ever been times when the teacher or you were uncomfortable with the apparently friendly rapport? Do you recall any teacher who appeared to be too friendly with the students? What was the effect of being too friendly?

9 A Field Trip Experience

PREVIEW

Some teachers believe that field trips are an essential part of students' learning experience. If a teacher works near a big city, there are bound to be significant museums, historical structures, and points of interest. For educators who work in small towns or insulated suburban communities, an effort to expose students to new environments will expand students' experiences. Of course, a field trip takes a teacher and students out of a daily routine and requires substantial planning. The teacher in the following case must decide if the trip she has in mind for her students is worth the considerable effort.

FOCUS QUESTIONS

As you study the following case, consider these questions: (1) How valuable are field trip experiences in general, and how important is the field trip that the teacher in this case has in mind? (2) In the following case, will all the difficulties involved in planning a field trip ultimately diminish its value?

THE CASE
A Field Trip Experience

Initially, Maxine Foley thought that teaching in the small town of Oakdale, near Big Pines State Park, would be peaceful and uncomplicated. Although her life did have these qualities for the most part, she had to confess that she also found her experience, far from the big city where she grew up, and the state university where she trained, to be often dull and boring. Oakdale featured a two-screen movie theater and a bowling alley. Most cultural events involved music and drama efforts at Oak-Ashton County Schools, where Maxine worked. Maxine had to admit that she was no Henry David Thoreau, and, while she appreciated the scenic beauty of the landscape around Oakdale, she sometimes needed the intellectual and emotional stimulation that one could find in larger communities.

One November weekend Maxine escaped 50 miles away to the significantly larger town of Barnhampton, lured by the attraction of the "Barnhampton Craft and Folk Festival." In Barnhampton, Maxine found the fried onion rings and funnel cakes unappealing and the hand-crafted lawn ornaments and bird feeders insipid, but she made a remarkable discovery. Maxine learned that Marjorie Haversford, a popular author of many young adult novels and poet of some standing in the region, had been born and had grown up in Barnhampton. Ms. Haversford's childhood home had been preserved as a museum, and Maxine delighted in taking the tour of the building.

To Maxine, the discovery of the Haversford Home was especially fortunate because her seventh-graders had just read the author's most famous work, *The Color of Sage Shadows*. In general, Maxine's students were not the most enthusiastic readers, but they enjoyed this novel and asked to read other works by the same author. As Maxine passed through the house and examined old photos and intriguing family artifacts, she thought, "Wouldn't my students just *love* this place!"

While talking to the guide/hostess at Haversford House, Maxine learned that outside of Barnhampton remained the "Station House," reputed to be a stop on the Underground Railroad before the Civil War. Not only did the house have historical significance, but it happened to be a setting for an episode in the Haversford novel that the students had read that fall. Before heading for Oakdale, Maxine investigated the Station House and was not disappointed that she had taken the time to do so.

Maxine recalled that many of her students had never been outside of Oakdale and had had very limited cultural experiences. As Maxine drove back to Oakdale that evening, she thought that her students might also be feeling bored and deprived. In their own backyard was the home of an author they admired. A visit to the Haversford Home might lend immediacy and legitimacy to writing as a career and to reading as a worthwhile endeavor. Very near their homes was a historically important house that remained as a vestige of a shameful period in the nation's history. Before she reached Oakdale, Maxine vowed that she would plan a full-day field trip and take her seventh-graders to visit the Haversford Home and the Station House in Barnhampton.

Maxine had never organized a field trip before. Since she was the only English teacher at the middle school and could not consult department colleagues, she turned to Ned Murphy, a veteran science teacher, for advice to learn the procedures for taking a field trip. Ned had taken a field trip 12 years ago and had only a vague recollection of the necessary steps, but he pulled down his faculty handbook and pointed out the procedures. Maxine would have to send a letter home to the parents or guardians to inform them about the trip and provide a rationale for its instructional value. She would have to secure the signatures of the parents or guardians and of other seventh-grade teachers on a permission form. Maxine would have to get two adults to help chaperone. She would need to type a list of names of all the students involved and submit the list to the attendance office 5 days before the trip. Ned observed, "The office will probably hassle you about getting a sub for the day, and the other seventh-grade teachers will be annoyed at having so many kids absent. Are you sure this is worth the trouble?"

Maxine contacted a person at the Haversford House about bringing a group of students on a tour of the home. She learned that the group rate would be $3 per person and the tour would last about an hour. Maxine realized that they could visit the Station House for free. She wanted the students to visit the fast-food restaurant that they frequently saw advertised on television. Lunch would cost each student about $2.75. The school had not budgeted for transportation for field trips, so students would have to pay for the cost of a bus for the day, at $270 per 5 hours, or $9 per student. Maxine calculated that the field trip to Barnhampton would cost each student about $14.75.

When Maxine described her plan to Gloria Hirschfield, the principal, she reminded Maxine that many families in the area were living on very low incomes and could ill afford to spend $15 on what they would deem a frivolous trip. Maxine wondered, "Isn't there some source to help out needy children? There must be some discretionary fund, or perhaps the PTA would contribute." Ms. Hirschfield responded, "Perhaps the PTA has money, but some families would choose not to let their child go rather than accept what they consider charity."

Maxine left the principal's office frustrated. At one point she thought she would take her students on a field trip even if she had to pay for it out of her own pocket, but apparently even that would not be possible. As Maxine walked to her classroom, she inventoried the many difficulties she faced in order to take her students on a field trip: compose an explanatory letter with a rationale and schedule, secure signatures on permission slips, collect money from and for each student, type a list of names for the attendance office, secure a substitute teacher and write sub plans, recruit chaperones, arrange for transportation, make reservations for the house tour, send a deposit, endure the disdain of disapproving colleagues, and negotiate costs with sensitive parents. Maxine recalled Ned Murphy's question: "Are you sure this is worth the trouble?" **If you were in Maxine's position, would you attempt to take students on the field trip?**

QUESTIONS FOR DISCUSSION

1. What tangible benefits, if any, are Maxine's students likely to gain if they attend her field trip?
2. Maxine seems to find the planning of the field trip rather daunting. Realistically, how difficult will it be to make the plans? What, if anything, can Maxine do to lessen her burden if she feels overwhelmed?
3. If Maxine must worry about the response of her seventh-grade colleagues, how can she reduce their possible hostility?
4. How can Maxine work with the financially strapped parents to accept the aid of the PTA, so that their children can go on the trip?
5. Maxine has anticipated a number of difficulties associated with the proposed field trip. What additional problems might she face before, during, or after the field trip?
6. In the end, considering all the challenges and the potential benefits, would it be worthwhile for Maxine to take students on the field trip? Why or why not?

RELATED RESEARCH AND WRITING

Select *one* of the following areas of investigation, research the topic, and produce a brief written report that you can share with your colleagues.

1. Identify a field trip experience in your area. Keeping a particular age group or class in mind, write a rationale and plan for taking such a trip. Check with a contact person at a school where you work or where you will have some clinical

or practicum experience, and describe the procedures that teachers at that school are obliged to follow in order to go on a field trip. In planning the trip, compose a letter to parents, collect any necessary permission slips and other forms, work out a schedule, determine the costs, and explain why the trip would be worth the costs and the effort.

2. If you are skeptical about field trips in general, write a brief report in which you explain the doubts you have. Recall any field trip experiences you have had during your time in school and explain why you found them of dubious educational merit.

3. Interview an experienced teacher about the field trips that he or she has planned. Ask the teacher to explain why he or she finds field trips worthwhile. How does the teacher select field experiences? To what extent do field trips pose excessive work for the teacher? Ask the teacher to describe one field trip that he or she found especially valuable. How did the teacher determine that students had gained something from the experience? Write a report based on your interview and share your findings with your colleagues.

10 The Perils of Technology

PREVIEW

There is no question that technology has had a profound impact on teaching and learning in America. However, the history of technology in American education has somewhat of a checkered past. Often reformers have latched onto technological advances as the solution to the ills of American education. For example, many reformers believed, as is true today with regard to computer technology, that television, and then video technology, were going to eliminate the need for teachers and classrooms. History has proven these predictions wrong. Now, television and video technology are tools that teachers use in the teaching and learning processes, but by no means have television and video taken the place of teachers. The following case brings into focus some of the conflicts that can arise as a result of the demands of new technology.

FOCUS QUESTIONS

As you study the following case, keep these questions in mind: (1) Should the teacher in this case give in to the demands that she modify her research assignment to satisfy the concerns of some students, parents, and administrators, even though she has concerns about the modifications she is being asked to make? (2) If a teacher changes an assignment because of a complaint, will she lose credibility with students? To what extent should teachers who are just learning to use technology be expected to implement and use new technology in the classroom?

THE CASE
The Perils of Technology

When Julia Cunningham, an experienced English teacher, distributed and explained her historical research assignment in her American Studies class, she felt pretty good about it. She believed that this revised assignment would solve the major problem she had had last year when she gave the same assignment. The assignment asked students to find historical information about one of the time periods that they had studied so far in the course—the Colonial Period, the Neoclassic Age, or the Romantic Movement—and to relate that information to the literature that they had studied. Or students could find biographical information about one of the authors whom they had studied from these time periods—such as John Smith or William Bradford from the Colonial Period, Benjamin Franklin or Thomas Jefferson from the Neoclassic Age, or Ralph Waldo Emerson or Edgar Allan Poe from the Romantic Period—and relate that information to the literature that they had studied.

This year the assignment indicated that students could not use information from the Internet. Julia emphasized this direction on her assignment sheet in bold, underlined letters, and she carefully went over this point in class. A few students raised questions and tried to get her to change her mind. Most of the students in the class seemed to be in agreement with the student who said, "All of our other teachers are *encouraging* us to use the Internet. It is so much easier to find information using it." Another student spoke up and said, "I don't understand why you won't let us use the Internet. I mean, the school is requiring all of us to learn how to use computers, so, like, what is the point if you won't let us use it for this class?" A third student added, "My brother took this class last year, and he said that his teacher let them use the Internet, so, if students could use it last year, why can't we use it this year?"

Julia was ready with answers to all of their questions. She told them that not all teachers were encouraging students to use the Internet, and she was one of them. She pointed out that, while it might seem easier to find information on the Internet, one problem is that much of the information that is available is not very good. She admitted that last year she had let students use the Internet, but she pointed out that students had not done a very good job, so until further notice the Internet was banned. While she got a few glares from a number of students, one student spoke up in support of the ban.

Julia spent the next few minutes discussing some of the excellent books the library had that dealt with the history of these time periods and the authors whom they had studied. She even wrote a few titles on the board and talked about why these particular books were excellent for this assignment. She was very hopeful that this would put an end to the poor quality of research that many students in the class last year had produced. It was clear to her that last year many students had simply looked up anything they could find, and it ended up in their papers. One student had even written a paper arguing that reports of Thomas Jefferson's alleged affair with one of his slaves was part of a communist-inspired conspiracy aimed at undermining the U.S. government by attacking America's patriotic heroes. The information was obtained from two questionable Internet sources. When she questioned the student who had written the paper, he seemed to be oblivious to the fact that his sources were highly questionable. The students in her class seemed to believe that if information appears on the Internet, it has to be true. Julia was sure that preventing students from using the Internet and requiring them to use books and articles that were readily available in the library would prevent this sort of thing from happening this time. When she had presented this change in her assignment to her history teaching partner, Joe Trumble, he had simply said, "I don't care. Do what you want."

Two days later, Julia received a parent phone call. The call came from Phyllis Taylor, Christopher Taylor's mother. Chris was one of the best students in her American Studies class. Ms. Taylor identified herself as a social studies teacher at James Madison Middle School, in the school district next to Julia's, and indicated that she had some concerns about the assignment. She explained that in her own teaching she tried to incorporate responsible use of the Internet into her research assignments. She indicated that she knew that there were numerous excellent historical sources available through the Internet, including university websites and a Library of Congress website. In fact, she briefly described an assignment she had her students do that asked them to find information from the Library of Congress website for oral reports related to ideas in their social studies textbook.

Julia told Ms. Taylor that she thought that was wonderful. She was glad that she had the time to show her students how to use the Internet. "Unfortunately," Julia said, "I don't have the time or enough knowledge to teach my students how to use the Internet. I have to get them through the 10th-grade American Studies curriculum."

"You know," Ms. Taylor replied after a long pause, "speaking as a parent in this community, I am also not very pleased with your decision. I have been reading articles in the local newspapers about how the district is spending a lot of money on new technology, offering courses for teachers to learn how to use the technology, and my son was required to take a course in computers. I just received a school district newsletter describing all the wonderful new technology-based programs in the district and the creative ways that teachers are using technology in their classrooms. Frankly, I am not very happy with this situation. I voted for the property tax increase for the school district to buy all this technology, and now you tell me that you won't let students use the Internet. Something is wrong here."

"I'm sorry you feel that way," Julia responded, "but I am not going to change my assignment." That was the end of the conversation. Julia knew that Ms. Taylor had made some good points. Julia supported the district's emphasis on technology. After all, she let students use the Internet last year, but it had been a disaster. She wasn't going to make that mistake again. Also, she wanted to take one or more of the new technology workshops that the district offered for teachers, but she coached girls' volleyball, was involved in curriculum work for American Studies, and had to have some time to herself to focus on her own family and raising her two children. There just wasn't enough time to do everything.

A few days later, on a Thursday evening, Julia got a call at home from her department chair. "I just got off the phone with Dr. Smith, the district curriculum coordinator," Dr. Marion Marchad said, "and he was quite concerned about an assignment you gave in your American Studies class. He said that a parent who is also a teacher at James Madison Middle School had complained about an assignment that her son had to do for your class and that you would not let them use the Internet. Is that true, Julia?"

"Yes, it is," Julia said. "But, did he know why I told my students they couldn't use the Internet?"

"No, he didn't. And that is why I am calling you. I want to support you, Julia. But this is a very difficult situation. Do you remember what I told the department at the beginning of the year about using technology?"

"Yes, I do," Julia replied. "Didn't you say something about the administration wanted us to make every effort to incorporate the use of technology into our teaching?"

"Exactly. In fact, I believe that I also asked everyone in the department to try and come up with at least one assignment that involved technology. Based on what I was told about this assignment, it sounds like a perfect one for having students use the Internet. And now I'm getting calls from the assistant superintendent, and he wants an explanation."

"I'm really sorry, Marion, but I have some very good reasons."

"Julia, I know it is late," Dr. Marchad said, "so let's talk about this some more tomorrow. I'd like you to come to my office first thing in the morning and bring the assignment you gave your students. Let's see if we can't find a way to resolve this situation."

Even though Julia was sorry that her assignment was causing difficulties for her department chair, she bristled at the thought that she should even have to consider modifying her assignment. After all, *she* was the teacher. She knew what was best for her students in her class. If she agreed to modify her assignment, she was concerned that she would lose all credibility with her students. Then, each time a student or parent complained about something, she would have to give in to his or her wishes. Unfortunately, Julia didn't have much time. She needed to give some further thought to this situation and prepare for her meeting with the department chair. **If you were Julia, what would you do? Should she try to think of a way to modify her assignment to satisfy her department chair, the assistant superintendent, Ms. Taylor, and at least some of her students? Should she hold to her belief that in this situation she knows what is best for her students?**

QUESTIONS FOR DISCUSSION

1. Should Julia give in and allow her students to use the Internet for the assignment she gave in her American Studies class? Why or why not?
2. If Julia decides that she does not want to allow her students to use the Internet for the assignment and explains her rationale to her department chair, what do you think will happen at the morning conference? Do you think Marion Marchad will listen to her reasons and then support her? Why or why not? Do you think the department chair should support her? Why or why not?
3. What other courses of action does Julia have in this situation? For example, should she discuss the problem with another administrator, such as the principal of her school, or would it be beneficial to seek help from other sources, such as her teaching partner in American Studies? Would any of these consultations be useful? What is likely to happen with each of them?
4. To what extent is the department chair, the school, or the school district responsible for the situation that has developed over the assignment in Julia's American Studies class? What else, if anything, could the department chair, the school, or the school district have done to better prepare or help teachers incorporate technology into the classroom?
5. What should Julia do? Why do you think that your recommendation is the best course of action for her to take?

RELATED RESEARCH AND WRITING

Select *one* of the following areas of investigation, research the topic, and produce a brief written report that you can share with your colleagues.

1. Investigate how a local school district went about acquiring and using new technology. Interview a district-level administrator, school administrator, department chair, or classroom teacher who was a part of the process. How does the administrator or teacher feel about the process? To what extent does the individual feel that he or she was involved in the process? What problems were encountered? How were these resolved? What is the current state of the project? Based on the information you have gathered, what conclusions can you draw? How might a district, school, department, or classroom teacher best proceed in learning about, acquiring, and then using new technology in the classroom? How might educators avoid the problems that occurred in this case?

2. Locate resources that can guide teachers and students in judging the accuracy and reliability of Internet sources for research. There are, for example, university Internet sites that offer guidance, and many writing handbooks discuss the topic. See, for example, Widener University's library website: http://muse.widener.edu/Wolfgram-Memorial/webevaluation/webeval.htm. Summarize the process one would take to judge the accuracy and reliability of information offered on the Internet. Describe a process for training students to evaluate data available on the Internet.

3. Contact a reliable spokesperson from a local school to learn about the school's "technology plan," if the school has one. How has the school planned for the use of instructional technology? Who was involved in the planning? What vision does the plan offer for the use of technology in the future? What inservice programs are available to train staff in the use of technology? To what extent is the use of technology an expectation for teachers?

11 *First-Day Woes*

PREVIEW

Even teachers with many years of experience often say that the first few days of class at the start of a school year or a new semester, particularly the first day, can be very trying. Often, the teacher does not know the students, and the students do not know the teacher or other students in the class. This is particularly true for younger students, especially ninth-grade students, who may be new to the school and to each other. How should a teacher, particularly a new teacher, start the school year in the best possible way? How can a teacher introduce the subject, the course materials, assignments, and teaching methods; establish school and classroom rules; and be true to his or her own beliefs about teaching? In addition, how should a teacher go about establishing a good classroom environment for learning and take into account the increasingly diverse student populations?

FOCUS QUESTIONS

As you study the following case, consider these following questions: (1) How can the teacher in this case balance the demands to establish course and school rules, introduce the subject of English and the content of the course, establish a classroom environment for learning, introduce his own teaching methods and himself, and have his students introduce themselves in a large class with considerable student diversity? In addition, how can the teacher balance all of these things in a classroom with some potentially significant physical limitations? (2) What should a teacher do to establish a classroom environment that is conducive to learning and to prepare a group of students for literacy learning at the start of the school year?

THE CASE

First-Day Woes

Mark Goodman was nervous but also quite excited as he and the other new teachers at Brookridge High School left the conference room where the principal and other school and district administrators had given them an introduction to the school and district and the school year ahead of them. Mark had been most impressed with the principal, Dr. Eugene Nesher, who talked about how important it was to get a good start at the beginning of the year. He had emphasized the need to establish a positive learning environment, and he had suggested that they all should become familiar with the rules and regulations for the school and go over them with the students in their classes. He had encouraged each of them to establish his or her own classroom rules with the students, and he had even handed out an article from a popular educational journal that discussed different strategies for management and discipline. Dr. Nesher had concluded his remarks by suggesting that, if they had any questions or problems, they should feel free to stop by his office and talk with him or one of the assistant principals.

Robert Meyer, one of the assistant principals, had distributed and reviewed the school rules. He had discussed some of the past difficulties with the tardy policy and had indicated that they really wanted to reduce chronic tardiness this year. He had encouraged the policy that students should be in their seats when the bell rings. Mark wanted to do his best to enforce school rules but he was beginning to worry about some of the things he was supposed to attend to at the start of the year.

As an English teacher, Mark had also been impressed with what Dr. Rebecca Zecker, the district curriculum coordinator and a former English teacher, had said to the new teachers about the importance of introducing students to the subjects and courses they would be teaching and even some of the teaching methods they would be using during the school year. As an example, Dr. Zecker had described an activity that she had used when she taught English. She started by putting students in small groups, a teaching method that she used frequently, and had them try to define English. Each of the groups reported their findings to the class, and then the class tried to arrive at a definition with which they could all agree. She also indicated it might be worthwhile to use one or two "warm-up" or "getting to know you" activities, especially for those who would be teaching ninth-graders, who are new to each other and the school. Dr. Zecker had described a "getting to know you" activity in which she went around the room and asked each student to introduce him- or herself to the class, to tell something about what he or she had done over the summer, and to describe a book the student had read. She had also pointed out that, even though this school year might be challenging for some teachers because the school was moving to full inclusion of special needs students, it would also offer new and exciting opportunities for everyone to learn to be more tolerant of those with differences.

When the meeting ended, Mark couldn't wait to get down to the main office and pick up his student class lists and get a look at who his students would be. He knew how important inclusion was, and he was excited to be part of something that he believed was the right thing to do. He was also eager to go through his files from his teacher education courses. Mark knew he had some interesting activities that he might use to introduce the subject of English and some of his teaching methods. He also knew that he had a set of classroom rules he had developed during a methods course, as well as two or three "warm-up" activities, also from a methods course. He was also eager to try out some of his ideas about management and discipline. For example, he believed teachers could manage their classrooms more democratically; he wasn't convinced that you had to assign students to seats, and he felt that they should have some say in deciding what the classroom rules should be. But, with classes starting the next day, Mark would have some work to do to prepare for his five classes and a study hall.

When Mark picked up his class lists—three sections of regular freshman English, English 102; two sections of regular junior English, English 302; and one section of freshman study hall—he paused in the office to study the classes and noted that his junior classes had 24 and 25 students in each, and two of his freshman classes had 27 and 28 students, but it was his first-period class that got his attention. He was shocked to see that there were 31 students in the class, and he noted a number of other factors that surprised him (see Figure 11A). He noted that there were two sophomores and one junior in the class and five students in his first-period class with various codes after their names. Mark carefully read what the special education codes meant at the end of his class list, and then he saw the attached memo from the chairperson of the Special Education Department:

To: Teachers with Special Education Students in Their Classes
From: Marion Vaughn
Date: August 16
Subject: Coordination with Special Education Resource Teachers

Welcome back. This is an exciting time for all of us. As you are all aware, this school year we will be implementing full inclusion of special education students into regular classes. You have one or more special education students in one or more of your classes. In addition to being enrolled in regular classes, each special needs student will be assigned a resource period to work with a special education teacher. You can identify these special students by the following codes:

—Physical Disability
*Behavior Disorder
**Learning Disability

You will be contacted sometime during the first 2 weeks of classes by the special education resource teacher assigned to each special needs student about the particular accommodations that are required for the special needs students in your courses. At that time, the special education teachers will discuss with you what they will need from you when they work with the special needs students. The Special Education Department is looking forward to working with you to help provide the best possible learning environment and support services for students with special needs.

The memo did not help Mark's quickly evaporating enthusiasm. From what he had learned in his teacher education program, he thought that inclusion meant that the special education and regular classroom teacher worked collaboratively in the same classroom. This situation seemed to suggest that the best he could hope for was that a special education teacher would work one-on-one with each special needs student during a period when the student was in a special education classroom. What really concerned Mark was that he had no idea what problems any of these students had. He was especially concerned about the student with a physical disability. What if the student was hearing-impaired or was in a wheelchair? What would he do and how would he handle it? Also, he didn't know how he would be able to handle so many students with special needs in this one very large class. Also, he wondered how he could make the course seem relevant to all of the students in class with so much diversity.

FIGURE 11A

First Period Freshman English Class

Brookridge High School English 1; E102; Section: 05; Room 111

Student	Class	Student	Class
1. Aguilar, Raphael F.	Fr.	17. Laponte, Maria S.	Soph.
2. Ankola, Ramesh B.	Fr.	18. Levin, Michele K.	Fr.
3. Bashir, Kristin L.	Fr.	19. Lopez, Arturo F.	Fr.
4. Blazyk, Lisa M.	Fr.	20. Martinez, Olivia M.	Fr.
5. Bond, John J.*	Jr.	21. Mulatz, Kevin A.**	Fr.
6. Chaudhari, Pratik	Fr.	22. Murphy, John C.	Fr.
7. Dembo, Laura M.	Fr.	23. Nelson, Derrick A.	Fr.
8. Ewing, Michael W.	Soph.	24. Nguyen, Tuan	Fr.
9. Frick, Lori P.	Fr.	25. Perillo, Jason S.	Fr.
10. Gennardo, Angela J.	Fr.	26. Sawicki, Elizabeth C.	Fr.
11. Grueneich, Kevin A.	Fr.	27. Schenk, Jonathan S.*	Fr.
12. Gutzmer, George H.—	Fr.	28. Sosa, Linda M.	Fr.
13. Handley, Clifford J.	Fr.	29. Utter, Robert M.	Fr.
14. Jakimiczyk, Mary S.*	Fr.	30. Vergara, Deanna M.	Fr.
15. Johari, Atul R.	Fr.	31. Yoon, William J.	Fr.
16. Kopterski, Richard J.	Fr.		

—Physical Disability
*Behavior Disorder
**Learning Disability

When Mark made his way to the classroom where his first period would meet, Room 111, and examined the room, he lost what remained of his enthusiasm. The classroom seemed small and cramped, and he counted only 29 desks. The walls of the room were made of brick, were a neutral color, and were completely bare of any decorations. In Mark's judgment, this was not a very good classroom for the group of students he was going to be faced with the next morning. He resisted assigning students to seats and even putting students in rows, but he couldn't see any other way to arrange the desks, and, with so many special needs students, he felt that he might need to assign students to desks. **If you were Mark, what would you do about the first-period class? What should he do the first couple of days of school about introducing and establishing the school and classroom rules; about introducing the subject of English, the course, himself, his students, and the teaching methods he will use in the course; and about establishing a climate for learning?**

QUESTIONS FOR DISCUSSION

1. Should Mark abandon the idea of establishing a democratic classroom or try to find a way to follow through on his beliefs, even with all of the difficulties he faces in his first-period class?
2. What, if anything, should Mark do about his shortage of desks and the lack of space in his classroom?
3. What are some things Mark can do to prepare for his special needs and repeat students in the class?
4. Given the large number of special needs students in the class, should Mark attempt to speak to the special education resource teachers immediately, or should he wait until they contact him sometime during the first 2 weeks of classes? What else might Mark do? How might that help?
5. From your own examination of Mark's first-period class list, are there other potential problems or issues that Mark should take into account in preparing for this class? What are these problems or issues, and what should he do about them?

RELATED RESEARCH AND WRITING

Select *one* of the following areas of investigation, research the topic, and produce a brief written report that you can share with your colleagues.

1. Do some reading on classroom management and discipline. What should teachers do at the start of the year? Why? Do some reading on establishing a classroom climate and introducing a subject, a course, and the social dimensions of the classroom at the start of a school year. What are some of the suggestions? Which seem most interesting to you and why?
2. Interview an English teacher about what he or she does at the start of the year. How does the teacher feel about establishing rules, assigning seats, and introducing the subject of English, the course, and teaching methods? What does this teacher do and why? How does the teacher feel about introducing him- or herself to the class and having students introduce themselves? What does this teacher do and why? How does this teacher feel about establishing a classroom climate? What does this teacher do and why?
3. Create your own activity or activities to introduce the subject of English and language arts learning, particularly course materials and assignments, and your own teaching methods. Invent your own "warm-up" or "getting to know you" activity or activities that will establish a good classroom environment for learning or help a class of students learn about one another. Design an activity that will help students learn classroom rules, such as procedures for speaking during class discussions or procedures for going to the washroom.

12 *First Observation*

PREVIEW

Most teachers find the process of observation and evaluation of their classroom performance to be very stressful. The visitation by a school administrator is bound to change the climate in the classroom, and it is hard to proceed as if no visitor were there. It is also stressful to think that someone will make a judgment about your performance and your worth as a teacher.

FOCUS QUESTIONS

As you study the following case, consider these questions: (1) How should a teacher prepare for a classroom observation by a school administrator? (2) Should a teacher adjust any plans and usual practices when the teacher expects a classroom visit?

THE CASE

First Observation

Lance Southey's department chair had already made one uneventful "informal" observation of his teaching; however, when the chair scheduled a "formal" observation in early October, Lance broke into a cold sweat. Lance did not see Helen Bastion, the English Department chair, as an aggressive, intimidating person, so at first it was difficult for him to understand his sense of panic about being observed and evaluated. Perhaps it was because he respected and admired Ms. Bastion that he cared a great deal about winning her respect, which placed inordinate significance on the observation.

As Lance reflected upon his reaction to the scheduled observation, he recognized several sources for his apprehension. First of all, three new teachers had been hired for the current school year. When the three teachers were hired, the personnel director noted that one position was a replacement for someone on maternity leave. The veteran teacher was sure to return after her 1-year leave of absence, and only two of the three new teachers could be retained. Lance felt that each observation would be a kind of audition for a job in competition with the other two first-year teachers. It also didn't help that Carl Cahill, an accounting teacher and notorious rumor-monger in the high school, made this comment about Lance's first observation: "You better watch out, buddy. Bastion is pretty tough. If she's determined to weed you out of her department, you're a goner. She's already driven a couple of people into early retirement."

Initially, Lance felt adequately prepared to teach high school English; however, when he talked to veteran teachers on the staff at Park Forest High School, he began to doubt that he knew much about teaching at all. Everyone else seemed very knowledgeable, prepared, and confident. Lance worried that, when Ms. Bastion came to observe, she would recognize his many pedagogical inadequacies.

Ms. Bastion had asked to visit Lance's lower-ability ninth-grade class, which met in the early afternoon, right after lunch. She scheduled the visit for a Friday during the school's homecoming week. This was apparently the only time that Ms. Bastion could schedule a visit in early October. Lance would have preferred that Ms. Bastion visit a different class, but he felt that he was not in a position to refuse. The class could be very cooperative and fun; however, on some days, especially after some distracting incident had occurred at lunch, the students arrived at class in a hyperactive state and could not settle down and focus on the lesson. Lance worried that the class could go either way—cooperative or wild. In fact, he assumed that Ms. Bastion's presence in the class would be enough of a distraction to trigger the students' hyperactivity. As Lance projected what he would be doing in class on the day of the visit, he recognized that he had planned a rather complicated structure to prompt students to discuss related themes in a series of poems.

Lance turned to two mentors for help. Arthur Jelinek was the "official" mentor that the school district had assigned to Lance as part of the formal mentoring program. Arthur had taught in the district for 30 years. Lance thought that Arthur was a very nice person, and he had been helpful in many ways at the beginning of the school year. For example, Arthur patiently reviewed practices in taking attendance, and he introduced Lance to the important persons he should know in the building. In addition, Elaine Kucnarczyk became an *informal* mentor. Lance gravitated to her because of her keen intelligence and pleasant demeanor. Lance felt comfortable in talking to Elaine about his lesson designs and about his concerns about particular students. When Lance shared his apprehension with his two mentors, each one offered advice about how he might approach his first formal observation and evaluation.

Arthur Jelinek counseled Lance in this way: "I'm going to tell you what to do. I can share with you a vocabulary activity that kids just love. Actually, it is a vocabulary *game*. It is all explained in a handout. Kids have to work together to complete the activity. The students will be *active*. It is just the kind of thing that Helen loves. The beauty of the vocabulary activity is that you can use it at any time. All students need to develop their vocabulary all the time. It's a sure-fire lesson. I'll put a copy in your mailbox."

Elaine Kucnarczyk suggested another approach: "Don't diverge from your instructional plan for the lesson that Helen will observe. Maybe you can meet with Helen before the observation to discuss your plan. She might be able to suggest some fine-tuning of the plan. Let Helen see what you can do, and let her make some recommendations.

I don't think you want to do something that wouldn't ordinarily be part of your lesson. Take some chances. Don't play it safe. Let Helen see you for the teacher you are. I know that you want to develop as a teacher, and it's Helen's job to support your development."

Lance was left with a few choices. He could play it safe and use Arthur's "sure-fire" lesson. He could take some chances by pursuing a lesson that is consistent with his over-all plan but might pose some problems for student engagement and management. He supposed that he could also approach Ms. Bastion about rescheduling the observation. **If you were in Lance's position, what would you do?**

QUESTIONS FOR DISCUSSION

1. Is it possible and advisable for Lance to try to reschedule the observation? What would be gained if he rescheduled?
2. What can Lance do to relieve the pressure of the situation enough that he can perform naturally and confidently?
3. Evaluate the advice offered by Lance's two mentors. Which mentor, if either, offers the most reasonable advice? Why?
4. What lesson options are available to Lance? Could he take an approach that Arthur and Elaine have not considered? What approach would that be?
5. To what extent has Lance placed too much pressure on himself? Is this actually a relatively inconsequential situation? Explain.

RELATED RESEARCH AND WRITING

Select *one* of the following areas of investigation, research the topic, and produce a brief written report that you can share with your colleagues.

1. Read the teacher evaluation plan for a school to which you have access. What are the steps involved in the evaluation of teachers? What criteria do evaluators use to judge the quality of a teacher's performance? Do the criteria make any sense as a standard for performance? What is the stated purpose for the evaluation system?
2. Search the professional literature to identify what other thinkers offer as indicators of quality teaching. Find at least three articles that describe exemplary teacher behaviors. Identify some similarities or recurring themes among the articles. Summarize your findings and share them with your classmates or colleagues.
3. Interview a relatively new teacher and a veteran teacher. Ask them to describe the teacher evaluation system in their schools. What has been their experience with teacher evaluation? Do they find the process a worthwhile one that encourages their professional growth? Do they view the process as an unnecessary intrusion? If they are rated, what is their reaction to the rating? Summarize what you have learned from your interviews and share your observations with your classmates or colleagues.

13 *Doing the Right Thing*

PREVIEW

While they may not receive the same respect or status as other professionals in our society do, teachers have a long history of being held to a higher ethical standard than professionals in other fields. For example, during the 1950s a teacher who became pregnant, even a married woman, was subject to immediate dismissal in many places in the United States. This case examines the ethical responsibilities of a teacher who observes another teacher engaging in unethical behavior and is encouraging other new teachers to engage in the same behavior. Under what circumstances must a teacher step in and put a stop to unethical behavior by another teacher?

FOCUS QUESTIONS

As you study the following case, consider these questions: (1) How should the teacher in this case respond when she encounters another teacher who is talking about one of her students in a derogatory manner and encouraging other new teachers to do the same? (2) To what extent does a teacher have an ethical responsibility to stop unethical behavior on the part of another teacher when that teacher is not directly involved in the unethical behavior?

THE CASE
Doing the Right Thing

When Rebecca Hart, a sixth-year English teacher, entered the teachers' lounge after her fifth-period class, all she wanted was a few minutes of peace and quiet during her preparation period before her last-period class. Everyone has bad days, and for Rebecca this had certainly been one of them. A fight had broken out in the hallway near her first-period classroom just before the bell rang, and she, along with another teacher, had had to break it up before anything serious happened. Fortunately, the two boys involved in the fight seemed to be more interested in acting tough than in actually landing a punch.

However, she ended up having to take the boys down to the office, and, as a result, her first-period class started late, and she had trouble getting the class settled down. Then, two periods later, a student set off a fire alarm, sending everyone outside in a cold, freezing drizzle for nearly 20 minutes. The next class period was a nightmare. She had trouble getting the kids in her ninth-grade "below average" class to settle down; when she finally did, it lasted for only a few minutes. She spent most of the period using just about every strategy she knew to keep them quiet and on task. As a result, by the end of fifth period, Rebecca was exhausted and ready for a little quiet time.

When she entered the teachers' lounge, Rebecca was a little disappointed when she saw that Lucille Browning, a veteran English teacher, was in an animated conversation with Mary Okawa, a first-year English teacher. Lucille could sometimes get loud, especially when she started complaining about things—the government, the school administration, and sometimes even her students. Rebecca's thoughts were on a quiet moment, so she headed for a chair as far away from the pair as she could reasonably get. Fortunately, there were only two other teachers in the lounge, so she did not have trouble finding a place to sit. Rebecca sat down and took a folder with some papers she needed to grade out of her briefcase and tried to focus on the paper on top.

"That kid's a jerk!" Rebecca overheard Lucille say to Mary.

"Really?" Mary inquired.

"And he's as dumb as a fence post. I really tore into his last essay. He can't write a simple English sentence. He's signed up for speech next semester, Mary, so, being our resident new speech teacher, you'll probably get him in your class. Watch out! He's a creep."

"He can't be all that bad," Mary said.

"Hey, Chuck! Don't you agree that this kid's a jerk?" Lucille suddenly shouted from across the room. "Isn't he in your biology class?"

Charles "Chuck" Castro, a first-year biology teacher, looked up from some student lab reports he was grading and somewhat hesitantly responded that the student in question was in his third-period biology class. Rebecca was more than a little irritated. She needed quiet, but, more important, she did not like the direction this discussion was taking. Complaining about her students to others was bad enough, but holding court with two impressionable new teachers was going too far. Also, encouraging Chuck to complain about the student was totally unprofessional. Rebecca wondered if it was too late to get up and leave before things got any worse.

"Come on, Chuck, admit it. The kid's a real jerk, isn't he?" Lucille prodded. "I bet he's pulled some things on you, hasn't he?"

"Well, now that you mention it, there was this one time when he and this other kid asked for a pass to go to the washroom and they were gone for most of the period," Chuck said.

"And what happened when they came back and you called them on it?" Lucille asked. "I bet he made some smart remark, like he usually does to me."

"Well, . . ." Chuck started to say.

Rebecca sighed and looked down at the paper she was attempting to grade, and she knew she would have to make a decision. **If you were in Rebecca's situation, what would you do?**

QUESTIONS FOR DISCUSSION

1. Rebecca is not directly involved in the conversation about the student, so does she really have a responsibility to say or do anything in this situation? Can't she just get up and leave? Why or why not?

2. Rebecca has had a particularly difficult day, and, given how her day has gone and her need to get herself together for her last-period class, should her most immediate concern be with getting ready for her class? Why or why not?

3. To what extent does Rebecca—or any teacher, for that matter—have an ethical obligation to take action when she sees another experienced teacher acting in an unprofessional manner in front of inexperienced teachers and encouraging them to act in an unprofessional manner?

4. While stopping what is happening now and immediately confronting Lucille with her inappropriate behavior might seem like the best thing to do, perhaps Rebecca should take her concerns to her department chair or another administrator. Would such a consultation be useful? What is likely to result?

5. Lucille complains about all sorts of things, so why bother saying anything to her about her inappropriate actions? Should Rebecca just take the two new teachers aside and tell them why it is inappropriate to make comments about students and to encourage others to do as Lucille has done? Why or why not?

6. What is the appropriate action for Rebecca in this situation? Why is that the right thing for her to do?

RELATED RESEARCH AND WRITING

Select *one* of the following areas of investigation, research the topic, and produce a brief written report that you can share with your colleagues.

1. Use an index of educational journals to search for articles that discuss professionalism and ethical standards for teachers. What standards do commentators offer to guide teachers in their ethical conduct in school and out of school?

2. Discuss with your classmates or colleagues their expectations for teachers' professional behavior. What kinds of behaviors do people find unacceptable for teachers? Guided by your discussions, devise your own code of ethical conduct that you can share with others.

3. Interview teachers, parents, and administrators who are connected with a local school or with the school that you attended as a student. Find out if the school does have expectations for teachers' ethical and professional behavior. For example, are there specific expectations for respecting confidentiality about grades, about medical conditions, and about other student records? Are teachers allowed to use students' written work in class to show examples of deficient performance? How do leaders in the school convey the expectations to the staff? What part do parents play in defining standards of conduct for teachers? Tell your classmates or colleagues what you have learned as an example of how a school might set standards for ethical conduct and train the staff in those standards.

14 *Copycat*

PREVIEW

It seems that every school has some trouble with students' plagiarizing. In some instances, the fault is the students' ignorance of the obligation to cite the work of another writer. The problem is especially troubling when a student intentionally represents the work of someone else as his or her own. Some schools provide rather rigid and clear-cut policies regarding the punishment for copying someone else's work. It is relatively easy to assign a punishment. The more difficult challenge is in training students to avoid plagiarism, to be sensitive to the need to attribute the work of others, and to gain the confidence to depend on their own efforts.

FOCUS QUESTIONS

As you study the following case, keep these questions in mind: (1) Is there anything positive that the teacher can do as the problem *develops* to diminish the impact? (2) What, if anything, should the teacher do to punish the student who you judge to be at fault in this case? (3) What long-term plan can the teacher put in place to help the student who has demonstrated a pattern of dangerous behavior? How can the plan help the teacher regain a positive emotional climate among the students in her class?

THE CASE

Copycat

While the other students in her senior honors class worked at their stations in the school's computer lab, Althea Zelknack shyly approached her teacher, Hilary Inglemeir, and asked in a confidential tone if she could speak to her alone in the hall. "Certainly," responded Hilary, curious to learn the need for Althea's secrecy.

In the hall, speaking in whispers, Althea started in this way: "Something happened over the weekend. I didn't know what to do. I told my mom. She said I should talk to you."

Hilary encouraged Althea to continue, expecting but dreading to hear some dark secret about Althea's personal life. Instead, Althea told this story: "On Saturday a few friends were at my house. We were hanging around in my room, talking and listening to music. That morning I finished a draft of the paper that is due for you next Friday, and I left it next to my computer, on top of the desk. After my friends left, the paper was gone. I thought at first that I misplaced it somewhere. So I thought, 'No big deal. I'll just print another copy.' But I worried a little that, if someone had taken the paper from my room and you saw a paper similar to mine, you would think I had copied it. I realized today that someone *did* take my paper. I know who it is."

"Who is it?" Hilary whispered.

"It's Wendy Rolfe," claimed Althea.

"How can you be sure it's her?"

"Just now, in the computer lab, I was waiting for my paper to come out of the printer. The paper that came out first, I thought it was mine, but it had Wendy's name on it. I read the first page and it was almost exactly the same as mine. I'm not a confrontational person, and I don't want to accuse Wendy of anything. I just thought you should know, because you'll probably get two papers that are exactly the same."

"Althea, thanks for letting me know. I'll have to wait until the papers are turned in; then I'll speak to Wendy. You just turn in your paper as you had planned, and don't worry."

While Hilary assured Althea, she had many doubts herself. Through the remainder of the class period, Hilary was distracted by the prospect of dealing with someone who had appropriated someone else's work. Hilary anticipated that in another week she would receive two almost identical papers and she would have to mete out some sort of punishment to one student for copying. One touchy problem was that Hilary could not prove to anyone that Wendy was the one who had copied the paper. Although Hilary believed Althea, the only evidence for condemning Wendy would be the claims that Althea had made against her. Wendy could just as well claim that Althea had copied *her* paper.

That night, Hilary couldn't stop thinking about the problem. She could well imagine Wendy insisting that she had written the paper she would submit in a week. Hilary thought Wendy was a nice kid, but she was very competitive about grades. Hilary could not imagine Althea lying to her or copying someone else's paper. The most disturbing aspect of the episode was that one student would intentionally allow her friend to suffer any repercussions that would result when the teacher discovered that someone had copied the work of another.

Hilary was hesitant to take any action. She didn't want to accuse Wendy of copying Althea's work, when Wendy hadn't yet turned in the assignment. Anticipating the possibility that Wendy would turn in a plagiarized paper, Hilary had to think of an appropriate response. Should she fail Wendy for the assignment and award no credit? Should she reprimand her and allow her to submit a new essay for partial credit? Should she refer Wendy to a dean, so that he or she could determine the penalty? Should she contact Wendy's parents to involve them in the punishment and intervention? How would Hilary even prove that it was Wendy who had copied Althea's work and not the other way around? As Hilary tossed and turned in bed, she hoped that Wendy would feel the bite of conscience and not turn in a plagiarized paper in the end.

During the following week, Hilary believed she noticed a definite change in the emotional climate of her senior honors class. Wendy's classmates seemed to distance themselves from her. Students avoided joining her for small-group work. She came to class alone and left by herself. She appeared to have no social interaction with the rest of the students. It seemed that the rest of the class had gotten wind of Wendy's indiscretion and had determined their own form of punishment. Hilary believed at this point that Wendy would get the message and not submit a plagiarized paper.

Two days before the essay assignment was due, Hilary talked to her colleague, Pat Ford, who had had Wendy as a student when Wendy was a sophomore. Pat said, "You know, her parents put a lot of pressure on her to get straight As. Her mom gives her a lot of incentives to get good grades—you know, shopping sprees at the mall, new CDs, and that kind of thing. I guess this has been going on for years."

"I'm really concerned," Hilary said. "It seems that all the other kids in her class are mad at her."

"It's no wonder," said Pat. "She's on a mission to become valedictorian at any cost. I heard she dropped her science class because she feared she would not get an A. A lot of kids think that she is not competing fairly with other students who are candidates for valedictorian, because she has fewer classes and an easier schedule."

"I'm afraid," commented Hilary, "that she has developed a pattern that could be disastrous for her future."

On Friday, when all the students turned in their papers, Hilary took the first opportunity to compare the papers of Althea and Wendy. They were almost identical.

Over the weekend, Hilary started grading the papers, but she postponed grading Wendy's and Althea's papers. Hilary knew she was procrastinating, but she needed some time to think about the problem thoroughly.

On Monday, Hilary arrived early at school and passed Wendy's locker on her way to her classroom. She noticed two poems taped to the locker—one, cut from the comic strip section of the Sunday newspaper, was written by children's book writer Jack Prelutsky; the other was a handwritten parody of the Prelutsky poem. The handwritten version, apparently intended to mock Wendy, read as follows:

Oh Essays, Oh Essays,
I hate you, you stink.
I wish I could stick you down in a sink.
Oh Essays, Oh Essays,
You're giving me fits.
I'm sick to my stomach and have
    a case of the sh_ _ s!

I'd rather go to prom with
    a bumbling dork
Than write my own essay,
    an original work.
I don't like you Essays,

So please go away.
And I really hate school;
I think that it's gay.

I don't want to go here,
But I must get straight *A*s!
So I'll copy all day
And I'll copy all night.
At least this one has no copyright!

Hilary knew that the poems were meant to attack and hurt Wendy, so she removed them from her locker. In the teachers' workroom, Hilary saw Pat Ford and showed her the two poems. "Oh, my God," said Pat. "This Prelutsky poem is the one that Wendy submitted as her own for our class poetry anthology in sophomore English. I remember because everyone liked it, and Wendy got a lot of attention for being clever enough to invent it. Some kid must have seen it in the paper this weekend and made the connection. It's too bad that Wendy feels she has to do this kind of thing. Her classmates are certainly on to her. I wouldn't want to be in Wendy's shoes for anything."

Hilary groaned. This seemed to be some corroborating evidence to prove that Wendy, rather than Althea, had copied the paper. Hilary had something tangible with which to confront Wendy. In a sense, she had "caught" Wendy and she could justify punishing her, but Hilary still wondered if that would be the right approach. Hilary knew she couldn't hold onto the papers forever. She would have to determine how she would contend with Wendy and how she would treat Althea. **If you were in Hilary's position, what would you do?**

QUESTIONS FOR DISCUSSION

1. How can Hilary adequately demonstrate to Wendy and her parents that she has done something seriously wrong? How will Wendy and her parents likely react?
2. Should Hilary punish Wendy? If so, what form should the punishment take?
3. To what extent does Hilary have a responsibility to protect Wendy's emotional state? What, if anything, can she do?
4. What actions should Hilary take in the near term and in the long run?
5. Should Hilary have acted sooner? What, if anything, could she have done?
6. What policies and/or procedures can Hilary put in place for the future, so that similar episodes do not occur again?

RELATED RESEARCH AND WRITING

Select *one* of the following areas of investigation, research the topic, and produce a brief written report that you can share with your colleagues.

1. Find out the policy regarding *plagiarism* at a school with which you are familiar. How is *plagiarism* defined? How are students taught about plagiarism and how to avoid it? What penalty do students face if they are caught plagiarizing? Do

individual teachers have the discretion to decide how to respond to each case? What changes would you make to improve the school's policy?

2. Discuss with a veteran teacher some experiences that he or she has had with students who have copied the work of other students or of published writers. What were the circumstances (e.g., the specific assignment, the time of year, the age, etc.)? How did the teacher treat the student? How did the student respond? Beyond assigning any penalty, what did the teacher try to do to discourage the student from repeating the same behavior in the future?

3. Examine several style manuals, handbooks, and curriculum guides to read a variety of policy statements about *plagiarism*. See, for example, the advice available at writing center websites, such as the one at Hamilton College: http://www.hamilton.edu/academics/resources/wc/AvoidingPlagiarism.html. Then devise a statement of your own. Have in mind students of a particular age. How do you define *plagiarism*? How can you model for students ways to avoid inadvertently plagiarizing? Share your written statement with your colleagues and solicit suggestions for revisions.

CASE

15 *To Think or Not to Think: That Is the Question*

PREVIEW

The myth is that teaching "honors" students is easy; they are smart and sophisticated, and they present few behavior problems. But, when the curriculum calls for teaching students critical thinking, problem-solving skills, and literature interpretation, the task can be quite difficult. The teacher in this case is confronted with circumstances that nearly every teacher must deal with at one point: Why won't this group of supposedly well-equipped honors students think critically? Her attempts to get them to work cooperatively, to discuss and debate important issues and themes raised in the literature, and to interpret the literature they are reading are frustrated at every turn. This case brings into focus some of the problems and issues that English teachers must contend with when attempting to teach students higher-order thinking skills.

FOCUS QUESTIONS

As you study this case, consider the following questions: (1) Should the teacher in this case keep trying to get her students to learn and practice the critical thinking and problem-solving skills that are important for students in honors and Advanced Placement classes? If she decides to continue trying, how should she proceed? (2) How does the teacher in this case contribute to the problems she is having in trying to get her students to think critically? What can she do to overcome these problems?

THE CASE

To Think or Not to Think: That Is the Question

Julie Benvolio was thrilled when she was told that one of the courses she was going to get to teach at John C. Fremont Memorial High School was 10th-grade honors English. She was especially pleased because she had heard that first-year teachers were rarely assigned honors students. When she raised concerns about her lack of teaching experience to the department chair, Steve Lyon, he dismissed them with a wave of his hand

and assured her that he thought she had excellent credentials and could do a good job. In fact, he said that one of the ninth-grade honors teachers described this particular group of students as "real go-getters," so she shouldn't have any problems. He told her that, if she did have any questions or problems, she should feel free to talk with any of the other honors teachers, or he would be more than happy to help her out.

When Julie met with the two other teachers who taught the course a few days before school started, the course leader, Jack Mathews, pointed out how important it was to emphasize critical thinking and problem solving in their teaching. "After all," he said, "these kids are honors students. Our goal is to make them independent thinkers and problem solvers. Remember," he added, "part of our job is to get them ready for the kind of critical thinking that will be required of them in the next couple of years, when they will be taking the AP exams."

The first few days of school, Julie was very pleased with how nice the honors students seemed. However, she had to admit that the department chair's description of the students as "go-getters" was almost comical. They came to class with sharpened pencils, and, if Julie made a comment about the weather, they immediately wrote it down in their notebooks and asked if her comment would be on a test. Her first couple of attempts at having class discussions were dismal failures. Julie would ask a question and then find herself looking out at a sea of puzzled eyes staring back at her, the students sitting quietly, with their notebooks opened in front of them, pencils in hand, waiting to write down her every word. Despite a vow she made to herself to make the students do the thinking and talking, she found herself answering most of her own questions. The students did fine in answering the literal questions, but as soon as she asked a question that required some thinking, the room suddenly became deadly silent until she relented and answered the question herself.

The results of her first few homework assignments and quizzes were also disappointing. Their written answers to questions were most often short and literal, but they were all turned in on time and were either neatly handwritten or typed. On the first quiz, many of the students earned a grade of *C*. When Julie handed them back, she got lots of complaints. Some of the students argued that the quiz had been too hard, and Mark Bertrand, who seemed to speak for most of the students in the class, complained that he didn't see how they could be expected to know the answer to at least one of the hard questions because she "hadn't gone over it in class."

The situation finally came to a head a little over a month into the school year, just after the class had taken their first unit test and when she had assigned them to read Kate Chopin's "A Pair of Silk Stockings."

"Are the tests graded yet, Ms. Benvolio?" Dave spoke politely as he and Jerry dashed through the classroom door.

"Yeah, how'd we do?" asked Jerry as they both walked up to her desk.

Julie replied, "Yes, yes, they're graded, but first we are going to examine that short story I asked you to read. So take your seats, guys, OK?"

As the two boys turned around and headed for their desks, they noticed the arrangement of desks in the room. "Oh, no, not again," moaned Dave under his breath.

Jennifer, who was one of the more gifted students in the class, and some of the other students were now entering the room. "Don't make us work in groups again, Ms. Benvolio," Jennifer moaned. "That wasn't fair last time when you gave us group grades. I mean, I did most of the work."

Julie knew that this period was not going to be easy. She purposely had put the desks in small groups before class because she did not want to give students a chance to get settled into their much preferred routine of taking notes while she talked. "Take any open seat you can find for now, class; once I take attendance and explain the activity I want you to do, I'll put you in the small groups I've assigned you to. I have your unit tests from yesterday, but I'll return them at the end of class, so we can focus on the activity I want you to do with the story."

"Could you please at least give us our test scores now?" begged Ann. Then, a chorus of voices joined in.

"How many got *As*?"

"What was the top score?"

"What was the average grade?"

"Please, class, not now. I said *later*. Everyone did fine, so relax. But I think everyone in this class can benefit from some practice that will force you to consider other opinions and discuss different interpretations, so we're going to work together today, in small groups, to do just that. Listen up for your name and the group I have assigned you to."

After the students got into their groups, Julie passed out the questions she wanted them to work on and announced, "Look carefully at the questions I have given you. Most of them ask for an interpretation. That is, the answers are not directly stated in the text. I want you to discuss and debate the questions as a group and come up with a group answer. I want one person to be the recorder and write down what the group decides. When you are done, we will discuss your answers as a class. Does everyone understand what I want you to do? OK, then, get started."

Julie stood back and let the groups work on their own for a while, and then she began circulating among the groups to check on their progress. She was dismayed with what she found. As she approached the group nearest the front of the room, she quickly discerned that no one was doing the assignment: two boys were discussing what they were going to do Friday night, one girl was covertly doing a homework assignment for her science class that was due next period, and another girl was just staring at the questions for the short story. Julie reprimanded the group and, after some further prompting, got them discussing the questions.

When she approached another group, she discovered that the entire group had let one girl answer all the questions for everyone. As she approached a third group, she saw one boy quickly shove something he was writing into his notebook and close the cover, and the rest of the group sat silently listening while two boys debated the answer to one of the questions. Julie encouraged other students in the group to speak up and express their views, and she moved on when it was clear that this group was finally involved in a group discussion. The last group appeared to be discussing something, but, as she got closer, she discovered that two girls were discussing a writing assignment for their journalism class, another girl was writing out the answers to the questions, and the rest of the group sat quietly, doing nothing. After some coaxing and cajoling, she finally got this group on task.

When Julie looked up at the clock, she realized that there were only a few minutes left in the period and that it had taken her most of the period to get the groups doing what she wanted them to do. She also knew that there would not be enough time to go over the group answers. Then, just when she was about to make an announcement, Jennifer interrupted her by asking if they would be graded on their group work. Before she could formulate a response, a chorus of student voices began complaining against group grades.

When she got the class quiet, Julie told them that they would finish their small-group discussions tomorrow and discuss their answers with the whole class. Then, she returned their tests and began reviewing one of the inferential questions a number of students had trouble answering. "Can someone tell us how he or she answered the question about 'Leningen Versus the Ants'? Do the events of the story support Leningen's lifelong motto, or do they reveal that it is not necessarily true? Explain." Julie looked around the room for volunteers but saw, from the expressions on students' faces, that she might easily wait until sometime next week.

"OK, then, listen," Julie began, offering them one possible interpretation, in the hope that it might prompt them to give another possible interpretation. Julie was finishing her response and turning it into a question: "So that is how the events in the story support his lifelong motto. But how might the events reveal that the motto is maybe not true? Could someone answer . . . ." One student, however, interrupted before Julie could finish.

"So if it is just your opinion, then one answer is as good as another!" someone said. "Anybody who has a reasonable answer ought to get credit!"

"Yeah! Everyone should get credit for an answer!" others said.

The bell rang before Julie could respond, and six or seven students started lining up at her desk as the rest gathered up their books and materials and headed for the door. As the line of students asking for extra points was forming, Julie wondered if there was anything she could do to get her students to think critically. **If you were in Julie's situation, what would you do?**

Questions for Discussion

1. Should the teacher discuss with the students the importance of incorporating critical thinking and problem-solving techniques in English? Why or why not?
2. To what extent is placing emphasis on individual grades and test points detrimental to the process of helping students learn critical thinking and problem-solving techniques?
3. Since the course is designed to prepare students for the Advanced Placement English Language and Literature examination, which is graded individually, is it fair to students to encourage them to work in groups during their English class? Why or why not?
4. To what extent is it fair and reasonable for Julie to assign students group grades?
5. To what extent is having students work in small groups helping them learn critical thinking and problem-solving strategies?
6. Why do you think Julie is having so much trouble getting this group of students to think critically?

7. Some might argue that getting this group of students to think is a hopeless task. Do you agree? Why or why not? Is there anything wrong with emphasizing objective information that students can recall? Explain.

8. What possible courses of action does Julie have at this point? For example, where else can she turn for help? What might she do in class tomorrow? How might this help solve the problem?

9. What is the best course of action for Julie? Why do you think that is the best course of action for her to take?

10. What lessons can be learned from this case? For example, to what extent should all students be learning critical thinking and problem-solving skills in English class?

RELATED RESEARCH AND WRITING

Select *one* of the following areas of investigation, research the topic, and produce a brief written report that you can share with your colleagues.

1. Read an article, book, or monograph about different approaches to teaching higher-order thinking, such as Leila Christenbury and Patricia P. Kelly's (1983) *Questioning: A Path to Critical Thinking* (Urbana, IL: NCTE). What are the strengths and weaknesses of these approaches? Which approach do you think would be most effective? Why?

2. Talk to a veteran honors teacher about problems he or she has had with his or her students. What are the major problem areas? Why? How did he or she address these problems?

3. Read a book or monograph about different approaches to teaching critical thinking and interpreting literature, such as Elizabeth Kahn, Carolyn C. Walter, and Larry R. Johannessen's (1984) *Writing About Literature* (Urbana, IL: NCTE) or Peter Smagorinsky, Tom McCann, and Stephen Kern's (1987) *Explorations: Introductory Activities for Literature and Composition* (Urbana, IL: NCTE). What are the strengths and weaknesses of the approach? How would you use these materials in your own teaching? Create an activity for a work of literature you are teaching based on ideas from the book.

4. Examine a book or monograph, such as Peter Smagorinsky's (1991) *Expressions: Multiple Intelligences in the English Class* (Urbana, IL: NCTE), that suggests ways to engage all students in thinking in the classroom. What are the strengths and weaknesses of the approach? How would you use these materials in your own teaching?

5. Check various websites to see how some educators define and promote critical thinking. One possibility is Montclair State University's Institute for Critical Thinking at http://chss2.montclair.edu/ict/. What do the several sites have in common in their approach to critical thinking? How do they differ? Based on your review, how do you define *critical thinking*? Describe an example of a classroom activity or experience that would fit your definition of a lesson that promotes critical thinking.

16 Do We Have to Read Huck Finn?

PREVIEW

This case centers on some important questions: What works of literature should students read and study in English? Why should they read and study them? How should the literature curriculum be determined? These seemingly simple questions are at the heart of this case, and, in a very real sense, they are the questions that have defined, at least in part, the teaching of English for the past 100 years or so. They are the questions that led James Fleming Hosic and a group of 65 English teachers who met in 1911 to form the National Council of Teachers of English, and they are the questions that have been discussed and debated at national conferences and seminars and among English teachers in English departments across the country. This case brings into focus some of the issues that English teachers must confront when attempting to determine what is the best literature curriculum for students and why. Curriculum development in English is not an easy process. It can be very difficult to sort through the issues and not lose track of the major goals of the curriculum, particularly when a single viewpoint seems to dominate the conversation.

FOCUS QUESTIONS

As you study the following case, consider these questions: (1) Should this teacher attempt to get his colleagues on the American literature curriculum committee to open up the curriculum to include literature other than canonical literature? If he were to make the attempt, how should he proceed? (2) If the teacher is successful at changing the curriculum, what problems will he and the teaching committee face in trying to move forward with the change? How can he and the committee overcome these problems? (3) How should curriculum decisions be made? What questions should be asked in developing a literature curriculum? Who should be involved in making curricular decisions and why?

THE CASE

Do We Have to Read *Huck Finn*?

Clarence Xiong felt very lucky 4 years ago when he was hired to teach English at Lake of the Hills High School. The school was in one of the most desirable neighborhoods of a large metropolitan area. Most of the students went on to college, and a fair number were admitted to some of the most prestigious universities in the nation each year. Teacher salaries were among the highest in the state, and the school district was in good financial condition. One of his teaching assignments was to teach the 11th-grade "regular"-level American literature course. Clarence was very excited about teaching this course that first year because one of his specialties was American literature, and one of the novels he taught had been his favorite in college, Mark Twain's *The Adventures of Huckleberry Finn*.

"Had been his favorite" is the operative phrase, because that first year and each year thereafter, Clarence's attempts to teach the novel turned out to be one failure after another, right down through this year. Although he had spent a good part of his summer planning a totally new approach to the novel, the results were no different than they had been in previous years. Now, he didn't even want to think about the novel or trying to teach it. In fact, his experience this year convinced him that the novel had to go.

Clarence tried a number of strategies to overcome the three major problems students had in trying to read and interpret the novel. One problem was that many students struggled with Twain's use of dialects. Many students maintained that sometimes trying to understand what Huck, Jim, and some of the other characters were saying was like trying to understand Shakespeare. Clarence tried two or three different activities to help students understand and work with dialect to better prepare them for understanding Twain's use of dialect in the novel, and, even though some of his students seemed to understand the dialects better after doing the activities, it was still a struggle.

In addition, many students and even some parents had trouble with Twain's use of the word *nigger*. Its appearance again and again throughout the novel made many students uncomfortable, particularly the two or three African American students whom Clarence had in each of his American literature classes. Again, he tried different strategies to help with this problem, but it just seemed to get worse each year. This past year, it was almost painful. The day he told the class that they were going to study the novel, they pleaded with him to assign them something else. Lisa Harvey, an African American student, seemed to express the idea that most students shared: "It's hard for us. The N word is ugly. Our parents and adults are always telling us not to use that word, and then here it is, like, on every other page or something. It is humiliating for me as an African American, and then you want us to talk about it all the time in class. There are some racial problems in this school, and this only seems to make it worse. Mr. Xiong, couldn't we please read something else?"

Related to Twain's use of the word *nigger* was the problem of trying to get students to understand his use of humor and satire, particularly in terms of important themes and issues, such as hypocrisy and racial prejudice. Too many students seemed to have trouble getting past a literal understanding of the novel. Part of the problem was related to

Twain's use of dialects in telling the story. In addition, students had difficulty reading the ironic tone. They had difficulty seeing the meaning behind the literal meaning of the words on the page. However, Clarence tried a new approach this time to overcome this problem, but the results were the same. Over this past summer, Clarence spent a good deal of time researching, reading, and planning a whole new approach to the novel. He came back with a new 7-week unit for *Huck Finn*. He had his students spend 2 weeks studying humor and satire before they even started the novel. He reasoned that, if his students understood how humor and satire work, they would be able to apply that knowledge to the novel, and they would be able to understand and appreciate Twain's humor, satire, irony, and themes. He tried to take his students' interests and abilities into consideration. They studied the humor and satire of stand-up comedians, such as Drew Carey, Steve Martin, Jerry Seinfeld, George Carlin, Chris Rock, and Bill Cosby, and they spent a great deal of time on some of the best of the Not Ready for Prime Time Players from *Saturday Night Live* and even some short works by Mark Twain and others. By the time they started the novel, his students knew what parody was, could explain how it worked, and knew what satire was and could explain how it worked. Clarence was excited. He kept thinking, this time it is going to work.

They started the novel. They looked at the opening chapters and identified some ways that Twain makes fun of society. Clarence got his students reading and talking about the Widow Douglas and her hypocrisy: She doesn't want Huck to smoke because it is a "mean practice" and "isn't clean," and, as Huck naively points out, "And she took snuff too; of course that was alright because she done it herself." After a day or two, Clarence began to have doubts when a few students had trouble with some of the satire after the opening few chapters, so he slowed down. He had his students look at Pap's bigoted, drunken tirade and Huck's moral dilemma. When he was sure they understood, the class moved on. Again, Clarence was feeling good. He had had a minor setback, but it had been easily and quickly solved. Now, he was sure things were going to be fine, so he assigned chapters 17–20 for the following day.

Then, before class the next day, one of his best students, Jennifer Sommers, came into the classroom and announced, "I just loved that poem we read last night."

"Poem?" Clarence said, at a loss for what she was talking about. He could not recall any poem that he had assigned. "What poem?" he asked.

"Oh, you know, 'Ode to Stephen Dowling Bots' that the character Emmeline Grangerford wrote. I didn't know Twain was such a wonderful poet," she added.

Clarence was sitting at his desk when this exchange took place. He thought about the verse in the novel, which is pure doggerel and intended by Twain to ridicule some of the sentimental verse of his time. He thought about the footnote to the poem in his annotated edition of *Huck Finn* from college: "Twain's parody of the lugubrious popular poetry of the time, such as the saccharine and atrocious verse of 'The Sweet Singer of Michigan' (Julia A. Moore, 1847–1920)." This student had obviously missed what he had thought was one of the most obvious parodies in the novel. Then, in all earnestness, Jennifer asked, "Are we going to study any more of Twain's poetry? I sure hope so. He's really good."

All Clarence could do was put his head down on his desk. At that moment, he knew that the rest of the study of the novel was going to go just about as it had been for the previous 3 years. *Huckleberry Finn* had been his favorite novel before he taught it, but now he did not want to even think about having to teach it again.

Clarence's problems with teaching *Huck Finn* were not his only major problems with the school since joining the district. Even though the school enjoyed a good reputation and had some excellent teachers, Clarence hadn't been prepared for the conservative attitudes toward curriculum that many of his teaching colleagues and people in the community shared. Clarence had gone through an excellent graduate English education program and had come to the school excited about trying out some new literature with his students, young-adult and recent American literature, and new approaches and methods to teaching. Unfortunately, he had discovered that most of his 11 colleagues who taught the junior American Literature course, many of whom had taught at the school for 20 years or more, were pretty satisfied with the course just as it was and saw no reason to change anything.

He was particularly surprised by this because many of them even talked about the changing demographics of the community. Twenty years ago, 94% of the population had been white. Now, the numbers were quite different and changing more each year. The most recent figures indicated that 69% of the population was white, 22% was African American, and the remaining 9% of the population consisted of a mixture of other minorities, primarily Asian Americans. What was particularly distressing to Clarence was that, despite the changing student population in the school, the literature in the 11th-grade curriculum had not changed at all in many years. There seemed to be very little in the American literature curriculum that spoke to the needs and interests of the growing minority population in the school and course. Other than a few modern short stories, the most recent major work in the curriculum was Harper Lee's *To Kill a Mockingbird*, which was published in 1960.

The few times that he or one of the other, usually younger, teachers had attempted to change even little things, a short story or a poem, they inevitably encountered a resounding "No!" from the majority of teachers on the committee, and even a little contempt from one or two teachers who seemed to believe that the traditional literature in the course was untouchable. Two years ago, in fact, when Angela Williams, who was then in her first year of teaching, suggested cutting one or two of the short stories by Henry James and adding some short stories by young-adult writers, such as Robert Cormier, Lois Duncan, Norma Fox Mazer, Walter Dean Myers, and Richard Peck, Dorothy Kronk, who was retiring at the end of this school year, had been so upset by Angela's suggestion that, after the meeting adjourned, she had followed Angela out to her car, haranguing her about the importance of having students "read quality literature that had stood the test of time."

Despite the claims by most of the teachers on the committee about how good the curriculum was, Clarence wasn't the only one having difficulties with teaching *Huckleberry Finn*. For the past 2 or 3 years when the American literature committee had had its monthly meeting following the teaching of the novel, a number of the teachers on the committee had complained about how badly the book had gone, again. Clarence had heard from one or two of his teaching colleagues that even more teachers were having difficulties with it this year.

Clarence was ready to try to do something about *Huck Finn*. He had thought a lot about it. He wanted to get rid of *Huckleberry Finn* and add a book such as Zora Neale

Hurston's *Their Eyes Were Watching God* or Alice Walker's *The Color Purple,* because both works dealt with some of the same themes, and both were by women and African American writers, which he thought would appeal to the growing numbers of minority students; whichever book they decided on, it would be a significant, well-respected work of literature that would make a good addition to the traditional American literature curriculum. Clarence knew that there were a few teachers on the committee who would support his proposal, and perhaps this year there would be enough teachers fed up with the problems with *Huck Finn* that they could change the curriculum.

Clarence had also talked with two teachers who taught the senior elective world literature course and had learned from them that, the way that course was set up, once each semester the teacher could pick from among three novels for students to read. In fact, they admitted that last year one teacher, Susan Morris, had let her students read any one of the three novels they selected, and she had run her class along the lines of a literature workshop while they read the novels they picked. Clarence wondered if one possible compromise might be to give teachers a choice between studying *Huck Finn* or studying one of the other novels he was thinking about suggesting as a replacement.

However, Clarence knew that, no matter what he proposed, getting the committee to consider doing something about *Huck Finn* was not going to be easy. He had to convince 11 other people to change. He was going to have to contend with some difficult and influential people, such as Ms. Kronk, who believed that *Huck Finn* was one of the major novels in the literary canon and had to be taught for that very reason. He knew that the committee members would point to recent research that indicated that it is the most taught novel in the high school literature curriculum. In addition, he knew that some of his colleagues were going to raise the "cultural literacy" argument. They would say that, despite the problems with teaching the novel, it was very important that students, particularly their growing minority population of students, read the great literature of Western civilization so that they learn the important cultural values and heritage contained in novels such as *Huckleberry Finn.* He knew that they had a point and that they would certainly argue that some parents feel the same way. Thus, even if he were to convince his colleagues to change, they would have to sell it to parents and the administration.

Furthermore, when Clarence mentioned the idea of replacing *Huck Finn* with something else to a colleague on the American Literature Curriculum Committee, Harry Stowe, a 20-year veteran, raised a strong argument: "Look Clarence," he said, "I agree that there are problems with trying to teach the novel, but we can't get rid of it just because it is difficult to read. If we are going to throw out every work of literature that is difficult, then what is left? Do we just pander to the kids and pick literature because it is easy to read and they like it?"

The more Clarence thought about all of the issues and problems, the more concerned he became. Another possible option was to ask his department chair to take him off the course next year and assign him to teach something else. The problem was that this solution seemed as if he were running from the problem. At the same time, he couldn't imagine having to teach the novel again. However, his chance to do something about the situation would come tomorrow after school, when the American Literature Curriculum Committee would have its monthly meeting, and the main item up for discussion was *Huckleberry Finn.* There were a number of possible solutions swirling around in Clarence's head as he walked into the English Office and headed for his desk, and as he sat down he hoped that a specific plan of action would take shape. **If you were in Clarence's situation, what would you do?**

QUESTIONS FOR DISCUSSION

1. What are the key issues presented in this case that Clarence is going to have to consider in coming up with a plan to convince his colleagues to change the literature curriculum?
2. Is Clarence correct in thinking that he must infuse the literature curriculum with selections from hitherto underrepresented authors or groups? Explain. Are the more experienced teachers correct in their belief that *The Adventures of Huckleberry Finn* must be taught? Explain.
3. Some might argue that getting the curriculum committee to change is a hopeless task, and Clarence would be better off asking his department chair to assign him to another course to teach. Do you agree or disagree? Why? What might be some of the negative consequences of taking this course of action?
4. What are some of the possible courses of action for Clarence? What are the strengths and weaknesses of these plans?
5. What is the best course of action for Clarence? Why do you think that is the best course of action for him to take?
6. Will the fact that Clarence is himself a member of a minority group hinder or help him in his quest to change the literature curriculum? Why or why not?
7. Who should be involved in making curricular decisions? Why? To what extent should the demographics of the community influence the choices of literature?
8. Assume that Clarence proposes a plan to the curriculum committee to change the curriculum and his attempt fails. What should Clarence do next? What other course of action might Clarence have for his own teaching situation? What possible good might come from failing to convince his colleagues to change the curriculum this year?
9. What lessons can be learned from this case? for new teachers? for experienced teachers?

RELATED RESEARCH AND WRITING

Select *one* of the following areas of investigation, research the topic, and produce a brief written report that you can share with your colleagues.

1. Interview a veteran teacher or department chair about how curriculum decisions are made in a middle school or high school English department. Who has input in the decision-making process? Why? What are the roles of various members of the community, parents, students, teachers, administrators, and the school board? How is the final decision made?

2. Examine the literature curriculum of a course at a school with which you are familiar. Carefully look at the rationale presented for the literature or determine the rationale from the department chair or teachers who teach the course. What are the strengths and weaknesses of the literature in the curriculum? What needs to be changed and why?

3. Discuss with a veteran teacher some experiences that he or she has had with attempts to change a curriculum in an English program. What were the circumstances and what was the process like for this teacher? What were some of the major problems involved? How did this teacher overcome those problems? What advice does this teacher have for teachers who want to attempt to change the literature curriculum in their school?

4. Review some of the critical literature about the ongoing debate about studying *Huck Finn* in the schools. See, for example, Gerald Graff and James Phelan's (1995) critical edition of *The Adventures of Huckleberry Finn* (Boston, MA: St. Martin's Press). Write a statement about your own position on the controversy, with a developed rationale for your position.

5. Examine some of the professional literature on selecting materials for the English language arts curriculum. See, for example, the National Council of Teachers of English (1996) *Guidelines for Selection of Materials in English Language Arts Programs* (Urbana, IL: NCTE). These guidelines are discussed on NCTE's website. Please go to http://www.ncte.org/censorship/ and select the Guidelines for Selection of Materials in English Language Arts programs link. Write an analysis of these materials. What are the key issues involved in selecting literature? What criteria should teachers use in selecting literature and other instructional materials? What procedures should English language arts educators use when selecting literature? What problems do you see in using these criteria and procedures? Why? What would you add and why?

17 *Call Me Irreplaceable*

PREVIEW

It is difficult for a new teacher to replace a popular veteran teacher. The replacement is naturally tempted to follow some of the practices that made his or her predecessor popular. It is understandable that a teacher wants to be liked by students and parents. However, popularity sometimes comes at a price when a teacher cannot find his or her own identity. In the following case, a new teacher follows a legend. While the new teacher would like to emulate some of the finer qualities of the veteran teacher, she knows it is impossible to do everything just the way the older teacher did.

FOCUS QUESTIONS

As you study the following case, consider these questions: (1) Should the teacher attempt to please students and parents? (2) Is it possible to satisfy students and parents and lose the confidence of colleagues? Whose judgment and sentiments should guide the teacher?

THE CASE
Call Me Irreplaceable

At Eleanor Keeneway's retirement party, Stan Lofton, the principal of Gresham Middle School, described her as "irreplaceable" and a "monument to middle school teaching." Parents, former students, and colleagues tearfully recalled special moments in the career of Mrs. Keeneway. Parents and students loved her kindness and her patience. She seemed to take a personal interest in each child.

    Colleagues had the impression that she somehow found the time to attend each music performance, athletic event, social function, and fund-raising activity in which her students were involved. Parents shared with each other the belief that students who had struggled academically with other teachers thrived in seventh grade under Mrs. Keeneway.

Mr. Lofton could recall no parent complaint about Mrs. Keeneway during his 10-year tenure as principal at Gresham.

When Mr. Lofton hired Ann Kobitz to replace Mrs. Keeneway, he warned her that she would be "filling some mighty big shoes." As a young first-year teacher, recently graduated from college, Ann was a bit intimidated by the challenge of replacing the "irreplaceable." She only hoped that everyone would give her time to adjust and not expect her to become a second Mrs. Keeneway.

At the beginning of the school year, Ann worked diligently to live up to what she believed was the Keeneway standard. She devoted hours to planning purposeful lessons, grading papers, and offering students substantial feedback on their work. She believed that she embraced realistic expectations, which she explicitly shared with the students. Ann attempted to make appearances at as many student activities as possible but placed her planning and assessment before her attendance at school activities.

By the middle of October, Ann had begun to feel the strain of her attempts to provide purposeful and engaging lessons, to read and respond to her students' frequent writing, and to support students in their athletic, artistic, and social development. There were times when Ann chose to meet family obligations or visit with friends, rather than attend another soccer game or choral concert. Soon Ann began to hear some grumbling among her students and a few complaints from parents. Students asked, "Why weren't you at the cross-country meet last night?" or "Why do we have so much homework?" One parent phone call resonated in Ann's memory. The parent said, "I've had three kids who went through seventh grade with Mrs. Keeneway, and they never received this much work or such poor grades." Even the librarian was critical of a complex research project that required the students to work in the learning center for 4 days and collaborate in teams of two or three. The librarian sniffed, "Mrs. Keeneway never would have done things this way."

In contrast, Mrs. Keeneway was not nearly as popular among the two eighth-grade language arts teachers. Jack Docent, one of the two teachers, observed, "I won't deny that the kids loved Eleanor, but I don't think she taught them anything about writing. She made the kids feel good about themselves, but she really didn't demand much. And Eleanor would be the first to admit that her primary concern was with protecting the kids' psyches. She saw middle school as a time for kids to grow up with their personalities intact. She was less concerned about attending to goals for reading and writing." Leslie Ward, the other eighth-grade teacher, complained, "She made our job much more difficult because a lot of kids coasted for a year and now have to do some work and learn to write. You can easily tell the difference between those students who had Mrs. Keeneway last year and those who had another teacher. We have to field complaints from parents because students now are struggling after they had great grades last year. Eleanor really put us in a vulnerable position. I really like Eleanor as a person, but I'm glad you have replaced her. It will make my job a lot easier."

Ann made casual discoveries about the nature of Mrs. Keeneway's instruction. At the back of one file drawer in the room that Ann inherited, she found stacks of ungraded papers and wondered if Mrs. Keeneway had ever read them. The audiovisual coordinator at Gresham asked Ann if she would need a video player and monitor in her room every day, as Mrs. Keeneway had in the past. An eighth-grade sibling of one of Ann's current students noted, "We never got homework last year. Mrs. Keeneway brought us doughnuts every Friday. She made learning fun. She was really cool."

Ann knew that she could not become a clone of Mrs. Keeneway. She was soon realizing that she could not be at every school event and keep track of every child. At the same time, Ann wanted students and parents to like her. She realized that as a nontenured teacher she would be vulnerable if parents started complaining about her to the principal, who appeared to have been Mrs. Keeneway's biggest fan.

In some ways, Ann felt like a victim of a fraud. She believed that she was now the target of criticism because her predecessor had pandered to children and parents. Ann's first response was anger, and she felt like exposing Eleanor Keeneway as an incompetent who had essentially been retired on the job. Ann thought that people should know, after all, what Mrs. Keeneway had really been like as a classroom instructor. Of course, attacking the popular legend would have its dangers.

Ann also thought that she might rethink her instructional approach, so that her performance standards were not so high and her homework assignments were fewer and less involved. She knew that, if she were more liberal with grades and homework, there would be fewer parental complaints, which would make a more favorable impression on the principal, who was her immediate supervisor.

There was approximately a month before the parent-teacher conferences that were scheduled on the days before Thanksgiving. Ann knew she would have to make some adjustments before she met with parents. She knew that she couldn't be Mrs. Keeneway, but what could she be? **If you were in Ann's position, what adjustments, if any, would you make in the next month?**

QUESTIONS FOR DISCUSSION

1. To what extent is Ann obliged to follow the examples set by Mrs. Keeneway? Does she have an obligation to please her students and their parents?
2. What are the many pressures that Ann faces as she defines her instruction and her teaching practices? Which pressures, if any, must she respond to?
3. Ann's eighth-grade colleagues expect her to improve on Mrs. Keeneway's efforts to prepare students to meet the expectations of the next grade. How fair and realistic are these expectations?
4. To what extent does Ann need to pattern herself after Mrs. Keeneway in order to satisfy her principal and get a good evaluation?

RELATED RESEARCH AND WRITING

Select *one* of the following areas of investigation, research the topic, and produce a brief written report that you can share with your colleagues.

1. View or recall several television programs or movies that depict the behavior of classroom teachers (e.g., *Good-bye, Mr. Chips, Dead Poets' Society, Up the Down Staircase, The Blackboard Jungle, To Sir with Love, Stand and Deliver, Dangerous Minds, Mr. Holland's Opus, Boston Public*). For your classmates or colleagues,

review a few of the films or TV programs about schools and teachers, and comment on the accuracy of the portrayal. What vision do these films or programs offer of the competent, loveable, and admirable teacher? Who is the unlikable and who is the despicable teacher? Do the images stand up to your experiences and your vision of a good teacher?

2. Talk to a few students of various ages and ask them who their favorite teachers are. What do they like about these teachers? Are there some common attributes among the favorites? Do the attributes represent characteristics that you aspire to have as a teacher? Share your findings and observations with your classmates or colleagues.

3. Recall a teacher whom you remember fondly and who had a positive influence on your life and your learning. What were the qualities that you liked in this teacher? To what extent are you able to emulate this person whom you admire? Is it realistic to think that you could be anything like the person who made such a positive impression on you? Share your story and insights with your classmates or colleagues.

18 *Evening Reveries*

PREVIEW

When a teacher cares at all about his or her students, the teacher experiences some emotionally wrenching situations. The teacher in the following case believes that he has encountered too many troubling stories, and he seeks relief. Is it possible to arm oneself against the emotional trauma that comes from learning about the lives of one's students? Is it possible, and advisable, to seek to work in schools where students seem to be relatively free of problems? If teachers feel an obligation to help others, should they seek to help where students are the neediest?

FOCUS QUESTIONS

As you study the following case, consider these questions: (1) To what extent is the teacher in this case facing a situation that is typical of most teachers? Will the current impact of the problems diminish over time? (2) What actions should the teacher take to help him cope with the current school year? What should he do about his future in teaching?

THE CASE

Evening Reveries

Mr. Wade Rivers slowly climbed the back stairs to his apartment after school on a gray Friday afternoon in February. Wade was usually tired on Friday afternoon, but today he felt completely drained of energy. After he entered his apartment, he dropped his briefcase inside the door, shuffled to the living room, and flopped onto the sofa. It was as if someone had pulled an electrical plug and cut off his energy supply. He had nothing left.

Wade fell into a deep sleep as the sun set and the room darkened. Two hours later, the phone rang and awakened him. He fumbled to put the phone to his ear and heard a vaguely familiar voice say, "Hey, where are you, man?"

"What? Who is this?"

"It's Kenny. I thought you were going to meet us at Jimbo's to go to the game."

Wade rubbed his eyes and looked around the room to find a clock, searching for clues to reveal the place and time. "I'm sorry, Kenny. I must have fallen asleep right after school. What time is it?"

"It's 7:30. We've got to get going. Are you going to join us?"

"I can't, Kenny. I'm just exhausted. You guys go ahead without me."

Wade hung up the phone and struggled to stand up and make his way to the bedroom. He wanted to go to the game, but realistically he had no energy to do anything but go to bed.

Wade assumed that he would just flop into bed and immediately drift into deep sleep. Instead, Wade tossed and turned. He couldn't help but review the events of the week at school. He realized that he could not easily discard recent revelations about some of his students. Clearly, the week at Pasteur Metro High School had taken an emotional toll on Wade. He abandoned for now the hope that he would soon fall asleep and padded off to the kitchen to make some tea. He turned on the heat under the kettle and waited.

As Wade sat at the kitchen table, he began to inventory the series of disturbing experiences from the week. On Monday, Wade had spoken to the school's social worker about Letty Piper. Letty was a ninth-grade student whose frequent absences and apparently chronic fatigue disturbed Wade. The social worker confided that she believed that the girl's mother had introduced her to, and more or less forced her to participate in, prostitution. Wade was outraged at the report and wanted the mother arrested, but the social worker noted that she had no substantive evidence to support her intuitions. The idea of the student engaged in prostitution was shocking to Wade. He thought that this student was still a little girl, and it was outrageous that someone within her own family was willing to put her life at risk in many ways in order to make some money.

On Tuesday, Wade saw three of his students in the custody of police officers who had handcuffed them and were in the process of searching them as Wade approached. The boys had been on their way to a confrontation with a rival gang, but someone had tipped off the police, who were holding the boys for carrying concealed handguns. Humphrey Wallace, one of the boys, observed, "I wasn't going to use the gun, Mr. Rivers. I just wanted to scare somebody."

The whistling kettle called Wade from his reverie. He selected from a jar a tea bag of something called Lemon-Lime Soother. That sounded promising—a "soother." Wade slowly poured the steaming water into his favorite mug, the one that had his university's crest emblazoned in gold on the side.

Wade waited for his Lemon-Lime Soother to steep, and his mind turned to reflections about another student. Wade had learned through a counselor that Atalanta Robbins, another ninth-grader, would soon be leaving with her family for Mexico. Atalanta was fighting leukemia. The family had tried several conventional medical treatments, with no success. When doctors predicted that Atalanta would soon die, the family sought help at a clinic in Mexico, where they would have access to medications that had not been approved by the FDA in the United States. The Robbins family took out a second mortgage on their modest home and sold many possessions to raise the money for the trip and treatment in Mexico. Wade did not share the family's hopeful outlook. He regretted that he felt certain that this gentle young student would not survive, and the family would return deeper in debt.

Wade sipped his tea and recognized that he couldn't help but bring home with him every day the stories of someone's misery, hardship, or catastrophe. This week's episodes in the troubled lives of Letty, Humphrey, and Atalanta were the latest installments in the continuous cavalcade of grief and squalor that Wade witnessed at Pasteur Metro High. If he delved at all into the personal lives of his students, he was confronted by an array of urban demons—teenage pregnancies, substance abuse, child abuse and neglect, gang violence, poverty, and fear and desperation.

Whenever Wade learned that one of his students was having a problem, he tried to intervene. He contacted the social worker, the counselor, the dean, the nurse, the police, the parents—anyone to find help for a troubled child. He learned quickly that most problems were complex, and his efforts to help were usually futile. He felt helpless, yet he worried about each child. The worry and disappointment were clearly taking an emotional toll. If Wade could objectively distance himself from some events, he could recognize that his work was important, and he could recall many success stories at Pasteur High; however, in light of recent events, he could do nothing more than to dwell on the negative.

At the end of the week, Wade thought, "That's it. I'm not asking any more questions. It doesn't pay to learn about the personal lives of these kids. I can't help, and I just suffer with them. Ignorance may not be bliss, but ignorance might help me to cope."

Wade recalled that he had trained at a university that was dedicated to urban education. Although Wade had grown up in an affluent suburb, he rejected the kind of regularity and homogeneity he saw in the suburbs. He was attracted by the diversity of the city. Wade felt a sense of mission in working in a school in the core of the city. He believed that the city's public high schools had long been neglected and needed the commitment of dedicated young teachers.

Wade drained the last drops of his Lemon-Lime Soother and recognized that he could not continue to absorb the repeated emotional shocks that were an inevitable part of life at Pasteur Metro High School. Wade knew he had to make a change, but he wondered what he could do. It was clear that, if he continued to work in the same place with the same approach, he would eventually experience some sort of breakdown.

There was no doubt about it: Life at Pasteur High was tough. It was part of a big urban school system. The complicated bureaucracy slowed action and made it difficult to get things done, even in getting books and supplies. The system made many demands on teachers to prepare students for various standardized tests that were intended to hold teachers and local administrators accountable for students' performances. Most of the students lacked motivation and came to high school woefully deficient in basic academic skills. Working at Pasteur was a challenge, and Wade concluded that knowing about the lives of his students and caring deeply about them was making his work tougher rather than easier.

Wade put his mug in the sink and made his way to the bedroom for another attempt at sleep. As he lay down and stared at the ceiling, hearing the muffled traffic noise from the street below his window and feeling the lonely crush of the consuming darkness, he thought that he had only two options if he were to continue teaching. He could shut himself off from any of the personal aspects of his students' lives. This meant that he would concern himself only with the life within his classroom and assume that everyone would have to leave troubles at the doorstep. He also thought about leaving Pasteur and finding a job in a less troubled school in an affluent suburb. One of his college classmates was already working at Bonnybrook Valley High School. She told Wade that there would be an opening there next year. She also reported that administrators at BVHS had high regard for graduates of the university that Wade had attended, and he was likely to be hired if he applied.

Wade wondered if he could really escape to a school where students had few serious problems. He also felt the pinch of conscience because he would be discarding his mission and abandoning those students who were in the greatest need of his services and talents. Wade wondered if he could realistically continue to work at Pasteur and try to ignore the troubling personal affairs of his students. Perhaps with experience he would become a bit more callused, so that each trial or tragedy did not carry an emotional burden. **What should Wade do?**

QUESTIONS FOR DISCUSSION

1. Is it necessary that Wade know something about the personal lives of his students if he is going to serve them as their teacher? Explain. Is it possible for him to remain aloof and ignorant of students' troubles? Explain.
2. Difficulties look especially grim in the middle of the night, when a person is fatigued from a tough week of work. To what extent might Wade be exaggerating the difficulties that he is exposed to? Are the problems likely to appear less significant to Wade the next day, after he is rested? Explain.
3. Is there anyone to whom Wade could turn for help? Who could he talk to? Would his university classmate at the suburban high school help? Is there someone at Pasteur High School who could help? How would any conversation with anyone else be of any use to Wade?
4. Do you agree with Wade that he has an obligation or a mission to serve the students in a very troubled environment? Why would he define this mission for himself? Does his rationale make any sense?
5. What short-term and long-term solutions can you devise for Wade? Imagine that you had to present Wade with some options. What rationale can you provide to support a particular course of action?
6. What hope is there for schools like Pasteur High School? Do the best and brightest teachers at such schools inevitably get frustrated and abandon the schools? What supports should be available to encourage talented teachers to stay?

RELATED RESEARCH AND WRITING

Select *one* of the following areas of investigation, research the topic, and produce a brief written report that you can share with your colleagues.

1. Talk to a veteran teacher about his or her views of the importance of knowing as much as possible about the lives of students. How does the teacher learn about

the students? How does information about their lives help the teacher with instructional planning? To what extent does the teacher attempt to intervene when he or she sees a need for help? To what extent does the teacher find that having knowledge about students' personal lives is emotionally taxing?

2. Read current reports about the state of high schools in the United States. What are the trends? Are schools safe? Are there significant disparities in the kinds of troubles that students face when one compares urban and suburban schools? Since all high schools enroll adolescents, the students experience the inevitable challenges of negotiating the dangerous ground between childhood and adulthood. Where do you see evidence that some schools have students who face egregious difficulties? Is there any way to predict which schools will have the most trouble?

3. Visit a representative urban high school. Spend the day in observing classes and in observing students in the halls and cafeteria. Talk to some teachers and students about what they like and don't like about the school. In the end, what is your impression of the school? Is it a place where you would want to send your own children? Explain. Is there any learning going on? Do students and teachers feel safe? Do students and teachers have a sense of pride in the school?

19 *When Do They Do Grammar?*

PREVIEW

It is not uncommon for someone to meet an English teacher and say, "Oh, I better watch my grammar!" The comment reveals an image held by some that an English teacher is someone who is very sensitive to the strict adherence to the rules of a standard way of speaking and writing and will publicly admonish those who violate the rules. The image also suggests that much of what English teachers do in the classroom is drill students to recall rules, to parse sentences, and to express themselves "correctly." In contrast to the popular image, it is more likely that English language arts teachers will eschew the drill in grammar and focus instruction on following a process toward the development of written composition. Critics, however, have wondered if this shift in emphasis has been a good one. In their enthusiasm for new methods for teaching writing, have teachers neglected instruction in grammar? Should instruction in grammar be a cornerstone of a curriculum for English language arts?

FOCUS QUESTIONS

As you study the following case, keep these questions in mind: (1) Are both the new teacher and the veteran teacher correct in their approach to English instruction? How can they both be right? (2) Would you agree that there is substantial evidence that the approach of the veteran teacher is an effective one for the teaching of English? (3) What different conceptions of language arts instruction do the new teacher and the veteran teacher represent?

THE CASE
When Do They Do Grammar?

During parent-teacher conferences in November, the mother of Grant Stuma asked her daughter's eighth-grade English teacher, "Is Grant supposed to be bringing home a grammar book? The only thing I see her bringing home is a paperback novel. When my son was in eighth grade, he brought home his grammar book and had homework every night. Some of the homework involved diagramming sentences. It was hard at first, but he got the hang of it and thought it was fun—sort of a puzzle. When do kids do grammar in your class?"

Leanne Stokowski, in her first year of teaching at St. Procopius School, attempted a summary description of her approach to teaching language and writing: "You see, Ms. Stuma, we study grammar, usage, and mechanics as part of the editing stage of the writing process. I am most interested in teaching students how to *write*, and research in the teaching of writing shows us that to drill in grammar doesn't really help students learn to write, so I don't have students do exercises out of a grammar text, but we do study grammar as necessary when we are editing our writing. I am most concerned at this point with the students' writing *fluency*, and I believe that their grammatical correctness will develop over time."

"I don't know," said Ms. Stuma, skeptically. "My son Nathan had Mr. Boswell for English last year, and Nathan has turned into a pretty good writer."

"I don't doubt that Nathan is a good writer," responded Leanne, "but I plan to teach writing as a thinking process, and I will focus on grammar and usage as a part of the process."

"I just hope," concluded Ms. Stuma, "that Grant will be ready for high school. I don't pretend to know the latest trends in teaching English. All I know is that when I was in seventh and eighth grade we did a lot of work in grammar, and that work helped me a lot in high school. Knowing grammar was a big advantage when I learned a foreign language, and I became a pretty good writer. I don't mean that I'm some F. Scott Fitzgerald or something, but I remember getting good grades on essays and compositions in high school."

Leanne thanked Ms. Stuma for sharing her observations about the teaching of grammar and tried to reassure her that she would not neglect her daughter's preparation for high school. After the conference, Leanne reflected on Ms. Stuma's remarks. As a graduate of St. Procopius School herself, Leanne had anticipated some conservative views among the faculty and parents. When she began teaching at the school, Leanne was confident that her approach to the teaching of writing, which did not rely on the study of grammar as the focus, was the right direction to take. She would just have to demonstrate over time that her approach was effective. It would take some time to educate the parents and win their confidence that her approach had some merit.

The comments offered by Ms. Stuma were not the first testimonial that Leanne had heard in favor of Mr. Boswell's approach to teaching English. Parents, students, and other teachers had sung the praises of Mr. Boswell. Franny Pastorelli, one of Leanne's colleagues, noted, "You have to admit, Leanne, Tom Boswell's students always do well on the standardized tests. I know that the achievement tests don't reveal everything about what students have learned, but Tom's kids always seem to score ahead of everyone else." Leanne had to admit that this was true. Furthermore, she was aware that last year two of Tom Boswell's students won the Writing Achievement Awards that were sponsored by the State Association for Teachers of English (SATE). The competition for the awards required students to produce compositions under timed circumstances. Apparently, Mr. Boswell's students could do more than just fill in bubbles on a multiple choice answer sheet. Parents were pleased that students who had had Tom Boswell for

English were sufficiently prepared to study grammar in the foreign language classes that they took in high school.

After hearing many testimonials in favor of Mr. Boswell's approach to the teaching of English, Leanne began to become somewhat resentful, because she equated the praise for him with some vague, implied criticism of her. At the same time, however, she found it impossible to resent Tom Boswell himself. He was a warm, compassionate, and generous person. Many students liked him because he took personal interest in each of them. He was positive and supportive. When Leanne started at St. Procopius, Mr. Boswell was quick to introduce himself and assure her that he was always available to assist her. He offered to share with Leanne any of the instructional materials that he used, but the material always seemed to be quite different from the emphasis and style that Leanne had chosen for her own classroom.

Leanne also recognized that Tom Boswell was not old-fashioned and narrow-minded. He was a member of professional organizations for teachers of English. He attended conferences and read the journals to stay current in the teaching of English. In fact, he had published articles himself and had contributed presentations at conferences. In general, colleagues from outside the school viewed him as a conscientious, reliable, and creative teacher. In school, everyone seemed to defer to the learned and erudite Mr. Boswell at meetings when issues about curriculum and instruction were discussed.

Students also held Mr. Boswell in high regard. They liked his class because they liked *him*. Students regarded his lessons as fun. Indeed, Leanne could see that he used a variety of games and cooperative learning structures as a means for teaching grammar. Sometimes Leanne's own students would ask, "Why do we have to *write* all the time? Why can't we do some fun stuff, like they do in Mr. Boswell's class?"

In the face of the many testimonials for Tom Boswell and in light of the mounting evidence of his effectiveness as a teacher, Leanne began to have some doubts about whether *she* was the one who was out of step with the best practices in the teaching of English. Upon leaving the university where she was trained in the teaching of English, with special emphasis on the teaching of writing, Leanne felt supremely confident that she knew exactly the right approach to language arts instruction. Now, however, as a practitioner in a school with other competent English teachers who had other reasonable approaches to teaching English, Leanne's confidence was shaken. She felt that *she* was the one out of step with the practices sponsored by most English teachers and by parents. She wondered if she should rethink the emphasis in her English class and pay more attention to direct instruction in grammar. After all, the emphasis on grammar seemed to be working for Mr. Boswell. **If you were in Leanne's position, would you change your approach to the teaching of English and place greater emphasis on the teaching of grammar?**

QUESTIONS FOR DISCUSSION

1. Is there reason to believe that Mr. Boswell's approach to instruction is more effective than Leanne's? What is the evidence?
2. If the practices in Mr. Boswell's class run counter to the training that Leanne received at the university, should she dismiss his approach as antiquated and useless? How can Leanne determine what the right approach is?

3. On a firm theoretical basis, judge whether Mr. Boswell's approach or Leanne's approach should yield stronger achievement among the students at St. Procopius.
4. To what extent should Leanne be guided by the preferences and observations of the *parents* in the St. Procopius community?
5. If Leanne doesn't change her approach, will she be isolated, and will she feel pressure to conform? Should any isolation or pressure influence her thinking?
6. In the end, what should Leanne do? Why should she follow the course of action that you recommend?

RELATED RESEARCH AND WRITING

Select *one* of the following areas of investigation, research the topic, and produce a brief written report that you can share with your colleagues.

1. Consult at least one study that reports the effect that direct instruction in grammar has on writing performance. Describe the methodology of the study and summarize the conclusions. To what extent are the results consistent with your own experience? What questions or reservations do you have about the study?
2. Read at least two journal articles in which teachers report their approach to the teaching of grammar. According to the writers, why is there a need and place for instruction in grammar? How do the writers suggest that English teachers should approach instruction in grammar?
3. Examine the approaches to the teaching of written composition that are sponsored by several influential thinkers (e.g., Ken Macrorie, Donald Graves, Lucy McCormick-Calkins, Nancy Atwell, Peter Elbow, George Hillocks). According to these commentators, what place does the study of grammar have in the whole English language arts curriculum?
4. Interview at least three English teachers about their experience with the teaching of grammar. How much do they teach, and when do they teach it? How do they teach grammar? After completing your interviews and reflecting on the responses, write your own position statement about the relative importance of the teaching of grammar in the entire scope of an English language arts program. Imagine that this statement would provide a rationale to parents and to supervisors to explain why you teach the way you teach.

20 *Vocabulary Wars*

PREVIEW

For years, educators have debated whether students should be taught to read and write through code-based (phonics, skills) approaches, which relate letters to sounds and sounds to words, or through meaning-based (whole-language, literature-based, emergent literacy) approaches, which do not dissect words and sentences into pieces but, instead, focus on the meaning of the text. The debate has become so intense that a few states have passed laws that give preference to (or even exclude) teaching practices based on one approach or the other. This case brings into focus some of the issues that English language arts teachers need to consider when attempting to decide how best to teach vocabulary. What approach or approaches should be the focus of instruction?

FOCUS QUESTIONS

As you study the following case, keep these questions in mind: (1) Which of the approaches to teaching vocabulary represented in the case seems as if it is the best one for the situation? Why? (2) What different conceptions of language arts instruction do the second-year teacher and the seventh-grade team leader represent?

THE CASE

Vocabulary Wars

The Metropolitan Area Reading Association (MARA) fall conference had been great. Rebecca Langer's school district had covered most of the expenses for her and three other teachers from each of the elementary schools in the district to attend the conference. She felt that she had learned a great deal. She had heard a nationally known expert speak about language acquisition and reading, and she had attended a number of excellent sessions by practicing teachers who had presented some interesting approaches to teaching reading, especially approaches emphasizing vocabulary improvement connected to what students are reading. However, the highlight of the conference, at least for Rebecca, had been the debate by two professors from nearby universities on whole-language versus phonics. The debate seemed to her to bring into focus some of the issues that were being discussed by teachers, administrators, and even parents at her middle school. Rebecca now felt that she could go back to her school with a better understanding of the issues, a broader perspective, and some exciting teaching strategies.

Rebecca was really looking forward to going back to school the next week. She wanted to share what she had learned at the conference, and she hoped that this would put an end to what she deemed the dictatorial approach to vocabulary instruction at Middlefield Middle School, which involved a daily dose of vocabulary workbook drills and memorizing "this week's 10 vocabulary words" each week. Rebecca was now in her second year of teaching at the school, and she had silently put up with the approach last year and had done what she was told, but this year she had begun to raise questions. What concerned her the most was that what she was being told to do in the classroom did not match with what she had learned about teaching vocabulary in her teacher education program. One day she had asked one of her colleagues, Sarah Chin, if she could identify who had selected the 10 words that students would memorize for the week. Sarah had just shrugged and said, "I don't know. I think these have been the 10 words for this week in the semester for the five years I have been at the school."

"Do you have any idea why the kids have to memorize these particular words? I mean, what do they have to do with anything?" Rebecca asked.

"I have no idea," Sarah replied. "I think I asked somebody once, and they told me that some of the weekly lists of words corresponded to the units they taught at one time, but we don't really teach most of those units anymore."

"Doesn't it bother you that we just have these kids memorize 10 words and their definitions each week and do exercises out of a vocabulary workbook, and there doesn't seem to be any connection to anything?"

"I thought that way at first, but I have found ways to connect some of the vocabulary words to reading and writing."

"What do you mean?" Rebecca asked.

"Well, two or three times during the year I have the kids write stories, and they have to use the 10 vocabulary words for the week in their stories. They seem to like that."

"That sounds good, Sarah, but I mean we do the same thing every week. They memorize 10 words and their definitions, and we do exercises out of vocabulary workbooks. There has to be more to teaching and learning vocabulary than that."

"You're right, Rebecca, but I'm not sure I want to fight with some of the other teachers around here who seem so committed to the current approach. It's just not worth it."

Rebecca had had similar conversations with other teachers, and that is why she assumed that Dr. Beverly Palinscar, the principal, had asked her if she wanted to attend the conference.

On Monday morning after the weekend conference, Rebecca approached Brad Johnson, her seventh-grade team leader, in the team office and launched into an animated description of the conference. She could not hold back her excitement. She concluded her monologue by saying, "I think what I learned is important, and I would like to share it with everyone. I think it could help all of us to reconsider what we are doing and not doing with vocabulary instruction to help our students become better readers and writers. I would even be willing to do a presentation for the teachers at our next curriculum meeting."

"I don't know, Rebecca. I can appreciate that you are excited about what you learned at the conference, but I've been doing this for a long time, nearly 20 years now, and it's been my experience that most of these professors at conferences have never been in a middle school classroom. Furthermore," Brad said—and she could see that the other team members in the office were secretly watching what was going on—"I think you'll find that most teachers around here are pretty satisfied with what we do with vocabulary. You may not find it all that exciting and interesting, but the kids learn their words and meanings, and the parents seem to like it. Maybe you should give some more thought to presenting what you learned to the other teachers."

"Maybe I didn't explain myself very well," Rebecca said. "The principal asked me to go to this conference, and I think Dr. Palinscar asked me to go because she knows that I am interested in vocabulary instruction. I'm not trying to destroy what we are doing with vocabulary. I just think that we can do more with it. We might want to think about adding some additional approaches, such as context and concept strategies, that research has shown help students read and write better."

"I've got a meeting with the principal later today, so I'll bring it up, if you insist. But I think you need to understand a couple of things. First, you really can't believe a lot of that research because it doesn't translate from one context to another: Just because something works in one teaching context doesn't mean it is going to work in a different context. Also, a number of teachers at this school spent a lot of time working on the vocabulary instruction we now use. I don't think it is right for you to be suggesting that we should change what we are doing before you understand all the reasons we do it this way. You may not realize it, but one reason we started doing vocabulary the way it is done is because our scores on standardized tests were going down a few years ago, so we looked at different strategies that could help us improve. These are the strategies that did it. I don't think our parents would like it very much if our scores on those tests started going down again."

"Maybe these strategies do help our kids do better on tests," Rebecca said, "but, the fact is, research indicates that it doesn't translate into any long-term learning. Kids forget the words and definitions soon after the test is over. So what good is it?" Rebecca said, raising her voice.

"I'm not going to let you denigrate memorization," Brad said, raising his voice as well. "We thought a lot about it and talked a lot about it before we did it. There is nothing wrong with having the kids memorize words and definitions. In fact, after reading some articles about it, we decided that kids ought to be doing a lot more memorization. It is an important skill."

"I really don't know what to say about that. I'm sorry, but I've got to go down and open up my classroom." Rebecca picked up her briefcase and materials for class and walked quickly out of the room. **If you were in Rebecca's situation, would you give up trying to change the way vocabulary is taught in the school and go along with the present approach?**

QUESTIONS FOR DISCUSSION

1. Looking at the testimonies presented for the two approaches to teaching vocabulary, judge whether the current approach or the approaches Rebecca recommends would be best for students at Middlefield Middle School.
2. The parents also seem to have a strong influence on the way vocabulary is taught at the school. To what extent should Rebecca be guided by the preferences of parents and scores on standardized tests in the Middlefield community?
3. What might happen to Rebecca if she continues to push for change? Will she be isolated? Should isolation or pressure from colleagues and/or parents influence her thinking and behavior?
4. What do you think would happen if Rebecca started teaching vocabulary the way she believes it should be taught? If Rebecca really believes that the other approaches are better, does she have a responsibility to do what she knows is best for her students? Why or why not?
5. Should Rebecca follow Sarah's lead and just try to find ways to make the current approach work for her in her own classroom curriculum? Why or why not?
6. If the practices in the school run counter to the training that Rebecca received at the university and what she learned at the conference, how can she continue to teach at the school? Should she consider leaving at the end of the school year?
7. In the end, what should Rebecca do? Why should she follow the course of action that you recommend?

RELATED RESEARCH AND WRITING

Select *one* of the following areas of investigation, research the topic, and produce a brief written report that you can share with your colleagues.

1. Consult at least one major study that reports the effect of whole-language or phonics on reading and/or writing. Describe the methodology and subjects of the study and summarize the conclusions. To what extent are the results consistent with your own experience? What questions or reservations do you have about the study?
2. Read at least two journal articles in which teachers report their approach to teaching vocabulary. According to the authors, how should English language arts teachers approach vocabulary instruction? What are the benefits of their approaches? Does an approach help students read and/or write better? Does it help students do better on standardized tests?
3. Examine what some influential thinkers (e.g., Nancy Atwell, Kenneth Goodman, P. David Pearson, Frank Smith, Frank Vellutino) have to say about whole-language and/or phonics approaches. According to these thinkers, what is the place of vocabulary study in the English language arts curriculum?

A Guide to Writing One's Own Cases

Anyone who spends a significant amount of time in schools will recognize tough situations and troubling issues that emerge on almost a daily basis. The cases contained in this book cannot represent all the challenging situations that a teacher might face and about which a teacher should be aware. The educational landscape changes constantly, and every school provides a unique context for teaching. It would be worthwhile for students and instructors to attempt to write their own cases after working with a few of the cases contained in this book. Our experience in working with case studies and in facilitating discussions suggests that, for any new case to produce meaningful discussion, it should have the following features:

1. There has to be a *central problem* that a reader can care about. The problem should be a significant one. A reader will judge the significance by seeing that there is a potential for a similar situation to confront any teacher. The reader will also judge whether the choices in the case can affect the teacher's career and can have an impact on several players in the drama.

2. The situation has to be *real*. There has to be sufficient detail, then, to make it real: Who are the characters? Where does the story take place? Why is there conflict? Where is there dialogue? There should be a level of recognition for the reader who is convinced that such events occur and could visit him or her.

3. The case has to *involve the reader*. What is the reader's role in the case? Is the reader in the place of the central character? Can the case's details help the reader feel a sense of urgency in taking some action? What should the reader do?

4. The case must make the problem an authentic one by including the *complicating factors*, so that it is not easy to arrive quickly at a simple answer. The case should represent the idea that choices have consequences and that some obvious choices are sometimes blocked by other pressures and circumstances. Most readers will figure out the easy problems on their own; the complicated problems are the ones that invite consultation with other thinkers.

5. The case should recognize that any group of educators are likely to represent *multiple perspectives*. Giving attention and respect to many points of view is a good habit of thinking to promote. The case will be richer if it can include several voices and recognize that there may be several legitimate and rational ways to think about the central questions of the conflict.

6. Describe the *procedures* that the readers should follow in order to think about the case, discuss the case, and write about the case. Readers might recognize that, as students, they were eager to know from instructors, "What are we supposed to do?" The case, then, should not baffle readers about the procedures but should suggest a process for working with the case and deliberating with others about how to work constructively to resolve the conflicts.

There are abundant sources for topics for case studies. If someone is already observing or working in a school, it is fairly simple to recognize sources of difficulty. If one were to return to the high school that he or she attended as a student, former teachers can tell stories about some of the concerns that they have had and some of the frustrations that they have experienced during their careers. No matter how intriguing an actual situation might be, professional integrity demands that one respect confidentiality and protect against compromising the reputations of any of the persons involved in the case. In writing a case taken from an actual experience, then, the writer will want to change the names of persons and places so that the case does not become an unchallenged attack on a person, school, or community.

If a group of colleagues or classmates were to produce a set of case studies, a pattern might emerge that could help one anticipate the major challenges that face the practitioner. Discussion about a variety of cases is likely to equip a teacher with the tools to work through some difficulties in order to concentrate on the rewards and the positive aspects of a teaching career.

About the Authors

Larry R. Johannessen is an Associate Professor of English at Northern Illinois University, where he teaches English education classes and literature courses primarily dealing with the Vietnam War. He holds a B.A. from California State University at Hayward, California, and an M.A.T. and Ph.D. from the University of Chicago. He taught high school English and history for 10 years. In addition to chapters in books, he has contributed over 40 articles to scholarly journals. He is author of *Illumination Rounds: Teaching the Literature of the Vietnam War* (Urbana, IL: National Council of Teachers of English, 1992) and co-author of two popular NCTE publications: *Writing About Literature* (Urbana, IL: National Council of Teachers of English, 1984) and *Designing and Sequencing Prewriting Activities* (Urbana, IL: National Council of Teachers of English, 1982). He is listed in *Who's Who Among America's Teachers* and *Who's Who in American Education*. His current research is in the areas of teacher knowledge and thinking, particularly for preservice and novice teachers; secondary school English curriculum and instruction; literacy learning; and the literature and film of the Vietnam War. He lives in Wheaton, Illinois, with his wife, Elizabeth Kahn.

Thomas M. McCann has taught English in a variety of school settings, including 8 years in an alternative school. He holds a B.A. degree from Northern Illinois University, DeKalb, Illinois; an M.A. from Southern Illinois University, Carbondale, Illinois; an M.A. from Saint Xavier University, Chicago; and a Ph.D. from the University of Chicago. He has published articles in *Research in the Teaching of English*, the *English Journal*, the *Illinois English Bulletin*, and *California English*. With Peter Smagorinsky and Steve Kern, he is the co-author of *Explorations: Introductory Activities for Literature and Composition, 7–12* (Urbana, IL: National Council of Teachers of English, 1987). He has taught for 4 high schools, 2 colleges, and 3 universities, where he worked with preservice and practicing teachers in graduate education programs. He has supervised teachers in high school for 20 years. As a department chair at Community High School in West Chicago, Illinois, he teaches English and supervises other English teachers. He also serves as an adjunct professor of English at Elmhurst College, Elmhurst, Illinois. He has collaborated with Larry Johannessen on research about the concerns of teachers during their formative years of teaching. He lives in Elmhurst, Illinois, with his wife Pamela and daughter Katie.

References and Related Readings

Atwell, N. (1998). *In the middle: New understandings about writing, reading and learning.* (2nd ed.). Portsmouth, NH: Boynton/Cook/Heinemann.

Bushman, J. H., & Bushman, K. P. (2000). *Using young adult literature in the English classroom.* (2nd ed.). Upper Saddle River, NJ: Merrill/Prentice Hall.

Calkins, L. (1986). *The art of teaching writing.* Portsmouth, NH: Heinemann.

Christenbury, L., & Kelly, P. (1983). *Questioning: A path to critical thinking.* Urbana, IL: ERIC/NCTE.

Cooper, J. M., & McNergney, R. F. (1995). Introduction: The value of cases in teacher education. In J. M. Cooper (Ed.), *Teachers' problem solving: A casebook of award-winning teaching cases* (pp. 1–10). Needham Heights, MA: Allyn & Bacon.

Elbow, P. (1981). *Writing with power: Techniques for mastering the writing process.* New York: Oxford University Press.

Elbow, P. (1990). *What is English?* New York: Modern Language Association and NCTE.

Elbow, P., & Belanoff, P. (1989). *A community of writers.* New York: Random House.

Fuller, F. (1969). Concerns of teachers: A developmental conceptualization. *American Educational Research Journal, 6,* 207–226.

Goodman, K. (1986). *What's whole in whole language.* Portsmouth, NH: Heinemann.

Graff, G., & Phelan, J. (Eds.). (1995). *Adventures of Huckleberry Finn: A case study in critical controversy.* Boston: St. Martin's Press.

Graves, D. (1983). *Writing: Teachers and children at work.* Portsmouth, NH: Boynton/Cook/Heinemann.

Grossman, P. L. (1992). Teaching and learning with cases. In J. H. Shulman (ed.), *Case methods in teacher education* (pp. 235–255). New York: Teachers College Press.

Hillocks, G., Jr. (1986). *Research on written composition: New directions for teaching.* Urbana, IL: NCTE/NCRE.

Hillocks, G., Jr. (1995). *Teaching writing as reflective practice.* New York: Teachers College Press.

Hillocks, G., Jr. (1999). *Ways of thinking, ways of teaching.* New York: Teachers College Press.

Kahn, E. A., Walter, C. C., & Johannessen, L. R. (1984). *Writing about literature.* Urbana, IL: ERIC/NCTE.

Lortie, D. C. (1977). *Schoolteacher: A sociological study.* Chicago: University of Chicago Press.

Macrorie, K. (1988). *The i-search paper.* Portsmouth, NH: Boynton/Cook/Heinemann.

Macrorie, K. (1996). *Uptaught.* Portsmouth, NH: Heinemann.

Maxwell, R. J. (1996). *Writing across the curriculum in middle and high schools.* Needham Heights, MA: Allyn & Bacon.

Maxwell, R. J., & Meiser, M. J. (2001). *Teaching English in middle and secondary schools* (3rd ed.). Upper Saddle River, NJ: Merrill/Prentice Hall.

Merseth, K. K. (1991). *The case for cases in teacher education.* Washington, DC: American Association for Higher Education and the American Association of Colleges for Teacher Education.

National Council of Teachers of English. (1996). *Guidelines for selection of materials in English language arts programs.* Urbana, IL: NCTE/SLATE.

Pearson, P. D., & Johnson, D. D. (1987). *Teaching reading comprehension.* New York: Holt, Rinehart & Winston.

Probst, R. E. (1988). *Response analysis: Teaching literature in the junior and senior high school.* Portsmouth, NH: Boynton/Cook.

Rabinowitz, P. J., & Smith, M. W. (1998). *Authorizing readers: Resistance and respect in the teaching of literature.* Urbana, IL: National Council of Teachers of English and Teachers College Press.

Rutherford, W. L., & Hall, G. E. (1990, April). *Concerns of teachers: Revisiting the original theory after twenty years.* Paper presented at the annual meeting of the American Educational Research Association, Boston.

Schon, D. L. (1983). *The reflective practitioner.* New York: Basic Books.

Smagorinsky, P. (1991). *Expressions: Multiple intelligences in the English class.* Urbana, IL: ERIC/NCTE.

Smagorinsky, P. (1996). *Standards in practice, grades 9–12.* Urbana, IL: NCTE.

Smagorinsky, P. (2002). *Teaching English through principled practice.* Upper Saddle River, NJ: Merrill/Prentice Hall.

Smagorinsky, P., McCann, T., & Kern, S. (1987). *Explorations: Introductory activities for literature and composition, 7–12.* Urbana, IL: ERIC/NCTE.

Small, R. C., & Strzepek, J. E. (1988). *A casebook for English teachers: Dilemmas and decisions.* Belmont, CA: Wadsworth.

Smith, F. (1982). *Understanding reading: A psycholinguistic analysis of reading and learning to read.* New York: Holt, Rinehart & Winston.

Spiro, R. J., Coulson, R. L., Feltovich, P. J., & Anderson, D. K. (1988). Cognitive flexibility theory: Advanced knowledge acquisition in ill-structured domains. In *Tenth annual conference of the cognitive science society* (pp. 375–383). Hillsdale, NJ: Erlbaum.

Spiro, R. J., Vispoel, W. P., Schmitz, J. G., Samarapungavan, A., & Boerger, A. E. (1987). Knowledge acquisition for application: Cognitive flexibility and transfer in complex domains. In B. C. Britton (Ed.), *Executive control processes* (pp. 177–199). Hillsdale, NJ: Erlbaum.

Sykes, G., & Bird, T. (1992). Teacher education and the case idea. In G. Grant (Ed.), *Review of research in education, 18.* Washington, DC: American Educational Research Association.

Tchudi, S. (Ed.). (1997). *Alternatives to grading student writing.* Urbana, IL: NCTE.

Vellutino, F. R. (1991). Introduction to three studies on reading acquisition: Convergent findings on theoretical foundations of code-oriented versus whole-language approaches. *Journal of Educational Psychology, 83,* 437–443.

Weaver, C. (1996). *Teaching grammar in context.* Portsmouth, NH: Boynton/Cook.

Wilhelm, J. D. (1997). *You gotta BE the book: Teaching engaged and reflective reading with adolescents.* New York: Teachers College Press and NCTE.

APPENDIX

Case Study Evaluation

Case title: _____

Date: _____

Directions: Please comment on the instructional value of the case study that you discussed. Your comments will guide the selection and use of a series of case studies that are intended for use in preservice and inservice training.

1. To what extent did the current case study generate meaningful discussion among you and your colleagues?

   _____

   _____

   _____

2. Please explain what important educational/instructional issues the case and discussion about the case raised for you.

   _____

   _____

   _____

3. To what extent did discussion about the case provide you with any insight into, or understanding about, important educational issues?

   _____

   _____

   _____

4. Please explain whether you heard any views during discussion that you had not anticipated or that you had not heard before.

_____

_____

5. To what extent did the case study and the related discussion help you formulate or reaffirm your views about the central issues?

_____

_____

_____

_____

_____

_____

6. Please explain what value, if any, the use of case studies of this sort might have in training prospective teachers and/or in supporting the continued development of practicing teachers.

_____

_____

_____

_____

_____

_____

7. Please note any additional comments.

_____

_____

_____